Advice from a Spiritual Friend

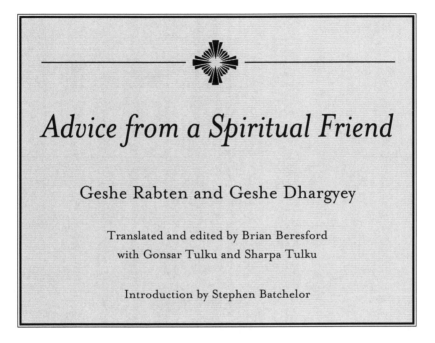

Advice from a Spiritual Friend

Geshe Rabten and Geshe Dhargyey

Translated and edited by Brian Beresford
with Gonsar Tulku and Sharpa Tulku

Introduction by Stephen Batchelor

Wisdom

Wisdom Publications
199 Elm Street
Somerville, MA 02144 USA

Library of Congress Cataloging-in-Publication Data
Rabten, Geshe.
    Advice from a spiritual friend / Geshe Rabten and Geshe Dhargyey ; translated
and edited by Brian Beresford with Gonsar Tulku and Sharpa
Tulku ; introduction by Stephen Batchelor.
        p.   cm.
    Includes bibliographical references.
    ISBN: 0-86171-193-9 (alk. paper)
    1. Atīśa, 982–1054. 2. Spiritual life—Buddhism. I. Ngawang Dhargyey,
1925–1995 II. Beresford, Brian C. III. Gonsar Tulku IV. Sharpa Tulku

BQ7950.A877 R33 2001
294.3′444—dc21   2001-022244

        ISBN 978-0-86171-193-2   ebook 978-0-86171-919-8

                21 20 19 18
                  5 4 3

Interior design by: Feron Design. Typeface: Mrs. Eaves 12/16.
Cover design by: Graciela Galup. Cover image courtesy of Virañani.

Wisdom Publications' books are printed on acid-free paper and meet the
guidelines for permanence and durability of the Committee on Production
Guidelines for Book Longevity of the Council on Library Resources.

Printed in the United States of America.

Dedicated to the long life
of His Holiness the Dalai Lama
and lamas from all the Buddhist traditions

Contents

Introduction by Stephen Batchelor. ix

Part One *The Jewel Rosary of a Bodhisattva* 1
    The Root Text 3
    The Commentary by Geshe Ngawang Dhargyey 9

Part Two *The Seven-Point Thought Transformation*. **47**
    The Root Text 49
    The Commentary by Geshe Rabten. 53

    Introduction 55
    1. The Preliminary Practices 59
    2. The Main Practice 69
    3. Changing Adverse Circumstances
       into the Path .97
    4. Elucidating a Lifetime's Practice 103
    5. The Measure of Having Transformed
       One's Thoughts 109
    6. The Commitments of Thought Transformation . . 113
    7. The Instructions on Thought Transformation . . . 121
    Conclusion 131

Appendix *Thought Transformation in Eight Stanzas* **133**
Notes **137**
Editor's Acknowledgments in the First Edition . . **143**
About the Authors. **145**

Introduction

In 1973, I was fortunate to have been among the small group of Westerners who were living and studying with Tibetan lamas of the Geluk tradition in Dharamsala, India, the capital-in-exile of the Dalai Lama. The teachings contained in *Advice from a Spiritual Friend* are translations of key texts of the early Kadam school of Tibetan Buddhism together with transcriptions of oral commentaries given by two eminent lamas, Geshe Rabten and Geshe Ngawang Dhargyey, in June and October respectively of that year.

Only fourteen years earlier, Geshe Rabten and Geshe Dhargyey had fled by foot over the Himalayas from Sera Monastery in Lhasa to escape the violent Chinese seizure of power in Tibet. While Geshe Rabten now spent most of his time in retreat in a small hut above Dharamsala, Geshe Dhargyey was teaching courses on Buddhism in the newly opened Library of Tibetan Works and Archives. Both were beginning to attract disciples from North America, Europe, and Australasia, most of whom had traveled overland to India and Nepal along the "hippy trail." Among them was Brian Beresford, a young photographer from New Zealand. With the help of Sharpa Tulku, who translated for Geshe Dhargyey, and Gonsar Rinpoche, the translator of Geshe Rabten, Brian assumed the responsibility of making these teachings available to a wider public.

Compared to the extensive literature on Tibetan Buddhism currently available in the West, little was then known of this profound tradition. Although a handful of classical Tibetan texts had been translated into English, they failed to communicate the vitality and directness of the lamas' oral instructions that so impressed those of us who were living around these extraordinary teachers. Lamas such as Geshe Rabten and Geshe Dhargyey made Buddhism come alive for us not merely by what they said but in the way they embodied it. Here were men who, overnight, had abandoned everything that was dear and familiar to them in order to preserve a vision of human life for which they were prepared to sacrifice everything. This was no dry theology we were studying but a passionate tradition of personal and social transformation.

Just as Geshe Rabten and Geshe Dhargyey sought to keep this tradition alive by communicating it to their young Western followers in India, it is fitting that the teachings of *Advice from a Spiritual Friend* have their origins with an eleventh-century Indian abbot who also walked across the Himalayas to bring those teachings to Tibet. This was Dipamkara Shrijñana, known as Atisha, who was born in Bengal in 982.

Atisha was not unfamiliar with arduous journeys. After many years of study and practice throughout India earlier in his life, he had a vision at Bodh Gaya (the site of the Buddha's awakening) of Dharmamati, a monk who lived on the island of Sumatra, in modern-day Indonesia. From his vision, he learned that Dharmamati was the only teacher who could convey to him the essential Mahayana Buddhist practice of *bodhichitta,* the mind that aspires to awakening for the sake of all living beings. So Atisha traveled for many months by boat to Sumatra and stayed with Dharmamati for twelve years. During this time Atisha received the oral traditions on cultivating bodhichitta. On returning to India, he transmitted these teachings widely, thereby reviving traditions that had been lost in their own homeland.

Atisha's fame eventually spread to Tibet, which at the time was undergoing a major revival of interest in Buddhism. Impressed by the extraordinary devotion of the Tibetan king who invited him, and despite the reluctance of his monastery to let him depart, Atisha left for Tibet in 1037 at the age of fifty-five. He remained there for seventeen years until his death in Nethang, just south of Lhasa, in 1054.

Atisha's mission was instrumental in laying the foundations for Tibetan Buddhism as we know it today. In the early eleventh century, Buddhism in Tibet was fragmented into conflicting groups of practitioners. While some maintained that strict ethical purity and rigorous intellectual training was the way to awakening, others insisted that only through mastery of tantric yoga could such realization be achieved. Atisha sought to reconcile these divisions by emphasizing how all these elements were equally necessary: without moral integrity and keen spiritual intelligence an effective tantric practice was impossible.

Atisha's primary concern was to establish a clear and pragmatic foundation for Buddhist practice in Tibet. Following the example of his teacher Dharmamati, Atisha instructed his Tibetan disciples in simple but powerful methods of thought transformation, which captured the essence of complex Buddhist ideas and served as pithy injunctions to effect profound changes in the way people thought and behaved. While some of these teachings were written down (such as the *Jewel Rosary of a Bodhisattva*, included with Geshe Dhargyey's commentary as part one of this book), much of what Atisha taught was transmitted orally to those who were deemed sufficiently prepared to put it into practice.

Widely regarded as the most succinct summary of Atisha's legacy, the *Thought Transformation in Eight Stanzas* was first written down by Geshe Langri Tangpa (1054–1123), to whom it had been transmitted by Geshe Potowa, a disciple of Atisha's immediate successor, the layman Dromtönpa. This text, presented as the appendix of this book, is a deeply moving reflection on the altruistic vision of Mahayana Buddhism. It shows how thought transformation is not merely concerned with improving the quality of one's own life, but requires a fundamental change in the way one sees and relates to others.

When the twelfth-century lama Geshe Chekawa (1101–1175) came across this text, he was particularly struck by the fifth stanza, which says:

> When others, out of jealousy,
> treat me badly, with abuse, insults, and the like,
> I shall accept their hard words
> and offer victory to the other.

In order to fully understand how to translate these challenging words into practice, he sought out Geshe Sharawa (1070–1141), a disciple of Langri Tangpa, and asked for instruction. Sharawa then taught Chekawa the *Seven-Point Thought Transformation*, which Chekawa subsequently committed to writing. It soon became acknowledged as the seminal text on the practice of thought transformation and was incorporated into the lineages of all the major Tibetan Buddhist traditions. Together with Geshe Rabten's oral commentary, it constitutes part two of this book.

The impact of Atisha's presence in Tibet was such that it gave birth to the Kadam school, which became renowned for the simplicity, integrity, and clarity of its teachings. Three hundred and fifty years later, the reformer Tsongkhapa (1357–1419) looked to the example of Atisha as a model for his own attempt to harmonize and syncretize the different Buddhist traditions of his day. Not only did Tsongkhapa regard Atisha as the true author of his (Tsongkhapa's) own key work, the *Great Exposition of the Stages of the Path*, but the Geluk tradition that was born from Tsongkhapa's teaching was also known as the New Kadam school. As lamas of the Geluk tradition, Geshe Rabten and Geshe Dhargyey thus represent a lineage that can be traced back through Tsongkhapa to Atisha himself.

These teachings on thought transformation are as applicable today as they were when Atisha first introduced them to Tibet. Although this complex, fast-moving modern world may subject us to greater levels of stress, the primary questions we struggle to resolve are essentially the same as those to whom these instructions were first given. Whether we find ourselves surrounded by a herd of yaks on the steppes of Central Asia or rush-hour traffic on a crowded freeway, we experience the same yearning to be free from the inner anguish of our existence and to find lasting peace and well being.

Thought transformation challenges us to recognize how much of our suffering is generated from within our own minds. Fixed opinions make us feel self-defensive and anxious; cravings make us feel frustrated and dissatisfied; hatreds make us feel irritable and tormented. To put these teachings into practice entails probing to the very roots of our habitual behavior in such a way that we can begin to change how we see ourselves and the world. The insights embodied in the pithy sayings of the Kadampa masters are like keys to help unlock the confusions deep within us. Teachers such as Geshe Rabten and Geshe Dhargyey were living examples of how such inner transformation was possible.

After we had received these teachings on thought transformation from these two *geshes* (a term that literally means "spiritual friend"), Brian Beresford dedicated himself to transcribing, translating, and editing the material. With the encouragement and support of Lama Thubten Yeshe, *Advice from a Spiritual Friend* was initially published in New Delhi in 1977 as the very first book produced by Wisdom Publications.

Two years after giving these instructions, Geshe Rabten left Dharamsala to become abbot of the Tibetan Monastic Institute in Rikon, Switzerland. In 1977 he founded Tharpa Choeling (now Rabten Choeling) in Le Mont Pelerin, near Lausanne, where he died in 1986 at the age of sixty-six. In 1983 Geshe Dhargyey was invited by his Western students to New Zealand, where he established Dhargyey Buddhist Centre in Dunedin. He lived and taught there until his death in 1996 at the age of seventy-one. Brian Beresford moved from India to England with his wife and two children in 1979, where he continued to work as a photographer and translator. He died in London in 1997 at the age of forty-nine.

The appearance of a new edition of *Advice from a Spiritual Friend* nearly thirty years after the oral teachings were given is both a tribute to the lives of these teachers and their editor-translator and an acknowledgment of the timelessness of the words contained between the covers of this book.

Stephen Batchelor
La Sauve Majeure

PART ONE

The Jewel Rosary of a Bodhisattva

Bodhisattvamaniavali

composed by the great Indian pandit

Atisha

with commentary
based on an oral transmission by

Geshe Ngawang Dhargyey

✦ The Jewel Rosary of a Bodhisattva

Homage to great compassion.
Homage to all spiritual masters.
Homage to the deities of devotion.

Abandon all doubts and cherish
    exertion for accomplishing the practice.
Abandon sleepiness, dullness, and laziness
    and always exert enthusiastic effort.
With recollection, alertness, and watchfulness
    always guard every door of the senses.
Three times during the day and night, again and again,
    investigate your mental continuum.
Proclaim your own faults
    and seek not mistakes in others.
Hide your own good qualities
    but proclaim the good qualities of others.
Reject acquisitions and honors
    and always reject desire for fame.
Desire little, be content,
    and repay acts of kindness.
Meditate on love and compassion
    and stabilize the awakening mind.
Avoid the ten unwholesome actions
    and always stabilize your faith.

Conquer anger and arrogance
and possess a humble mind.
Avoid wrong livelihoods
and live a life of truth.
Abandon all worldly possessions
and be adorned by the gems of superiors.
Abandon all frivolities
and abide in solitude.
Abandon all senseless talk
and always control your speech.
When seeing your master or teacher,
perform services with respect.
Toward a person having the eye of the doctrine
and toward sentient beings who are beginners
develop the recognition of them as teachers.
When seeing any sentient beings, develop
the recognition of them as parents and children.
Abandon misleading friends
and rely on virtuous spiritual companions.
Abandon minds of anger and unhappiness,
and wherever you go be happy.
Abandon attachment to everything
and abide free from attachment.
Attachment will never procure you a happy rebirth;
it kills the life of liberation.
Wherever you see practices leading to happiness,
always exert effort in them.
Whatever you have started to do,
accomplish that very thing first.

Do everything well in this way,
  otherwise nothing will be achieved.
Always be apart from liking evil.
Whenever a pompous mind arises,
  flatten such arrogance.
Recall the teachings of your master.
When a cowardly mind arises,
  praise the sublimity of the mind.
Whenever objects of attraction or aversion arise,
  meditate on the emptiness of both;
  view them as illusions and emanations.
When hearing any offensive words,
  view them as an echo.
When your body is afflicted by harm,
  view this as your previous actions.
Abide well in solitude, beyond town limits,
  like the corpses of wild game.
Be by yourself, conceal yourself,
  and dwell without attachment.
Always stabilize awareness of your *yidam* and,
  whenever laziness or lassitude arise,
  enumerate these faults to yourself
  and feel remorse from your heart.
If you see others,
  speak calmly and sincerely.
Avoid a wrathful and frowning expression
  and always remain cheerful.
When seeing others, continuously
  be pleased to give without being miserly.

Discard all jealousy.
To protect the mind of another,
   avoid all conflict
   and always have patience.
Do not be fickle or a flatterer,
   but always be capable of remaining steadfast.
Avoid belittling others and
   remain respectful in your manners.
When giving advice to others,
   have compassion and thoughts for their benefit.
Do not disparage spiritual doctrines
   and be intent on whichever you admire.
Through the door of the ten Dharma practices,
   exert effort throughout both day and night.
Whatever virtues are collected during the three times,
   dedicate them for the unsurpassable great awakening.
Distribute your merit for all sentient beings.
Always offer the seven-limbed prayer
   and great aspirations for the path.
If you act in this way, the two accumulations
   of merit and wisdom will be accomplished.
Also, with the eradication of the two obscurations,
   thus fulfilling the purpose of having gained a
   human form, unsurpassable full awakening will
   be achieved.
The gem of faith, the gem of ethics,
   the gem of generosity, the gem of hearing,
   the gem of consideration,
   the gem of shame, and the gem of intelligence:
   these are the seven supreme gems.

These seven gems are never exhausted.

Do not tell this to nonhumans.

Examine your speech when amid many people.

Examine your mind when living alone.

This has been composed by the Indian master
Dipamkara Shrijñana, the Glorious Illuminator,
the Essence of Primordial Awareness.

Translated from the Tibetan by
Sharpa Tulku and Brian Beresford.

THE COMMENTARY TO

The Jewel Rosary of a Bodhisattva

Homage to great compassion.
Homage to all spiritual masters.
Homage to the deities of devotion.

This short text by Atisha contains one hundred and eleven lines of advice in connection with the practice of thought transformation. It begins with obeisance to great compassion because this is the source of the many manifestations of a fully awakened being. The next obeisance to the spiritual masters implies that all inner development and experience is based upon devotion and confidence in the teachers of the path. This is the foundation for all successful spiritual practice. Both Naropa and his teacher Tilopa have said that without spiritual guidance there could be no fully awakened state. Lastly, obeisance is made to the deities of devotion (*yidam*). These are reflections of specific aspects of the awakened mind and are called upon when we wish to bring out these aspects in ourselves. For instance, when meditating to generate the conventional awakening mind, we should devote ourselves to Avalokiteshvara, the embodiment of compassion, and when meditating on emptiness, to Manjushri, the embodiment of intelligent awareness, or wisdom.

Abandon all doubts and cherish exertion for
accomplishing the practice.

Whatever our object of meditation may be, we must learn about it thoroughly beforehand and eliminate any doubts we may have concerning the procedures. If our teacher says merely, "Meditate on emptiness," and we leave without studying what was meant, we shall not know what to do. We may meditate by thinking about an empty room, having no clear idea what is being negated by emptiness. Thus, we must first learn about the meditation we wish to do and gain a precise intellectual understanding of it. Based on this, we shall eventually be able to transcend the intellectual level and meditate nonconceptually.

This line further implies that we should not become distracted, but meditate single-pointedly without any mental wandering. Moreover, the method we choose must be valid, and we must be convinced of its validity. Then, free from all doubts, we shall be able to meditate with strict concentration, confident that the path we have chosen is nondeceptive. We should not be like water on a tabletop, which can be led by the finger in any direction, easily swayed back and forth by the various opinions of others. We should know how to differentiate between valid and invalid spiritual teachings and be certain about what is right, leaving no room for doubts. If we apply the forces of hearing, or study, and contemplation, or examination, we shall be able to eliminate all indecisiveness.

Yet this is not enough. If we acquire sufficient intellectual knowledge about the meditation but never practice it, we are like a person who stores away food but never eats it. Such food will either rot or be eaten by rats, or the person will die without having ever tasted it. Tsongkhapa said that the purpose of hearing and acquiring intellectual knowledge is to meditate upon it. Therefore, according to our different levels of ability, we should hear and study the teachings as much as we can in order to meditate on or actualize them.

Because each person has different idiosyncrasies and abilities, everyone will not become enlightened as if stamped from the same mold. Bearing this in mind, we should practice in the way best suited to each of us. Without practicing what we have learned, we are like museum guides who know much but for whom the objects on display have no special significance. When we practice, it is important not to pattern ourselves on others; instead we each should examine our own abilities and meditate accordingly. To do otherwise leads only to frustration.

*Abandon sleepiness, dullness, and laziness
and always exert enthusiastic effort.*

We should eliminate laziness, mental wandering, mental dullness, and other such hindrances to our meditation, otherwise we may begin meditating with our head held erect, but later we will find it slouched against the middle of our body with our meditation turned to sleep. This line in the text is not belittling us but is a warning to arouse our energy for venturing into the practices. Even if we guard against all these obstacles, we must still have strong perseverance and diligence so that our meditation will be successful. As Tsongkhapa has said, "Wear the protective armor of enthusiastic perseverance and increase it like the waxing moon."

Also, Chandrakirti said, "All profound and superficial goals follow from enthusiastic perseverance; with it anything can be accomplished."

*With recollection, alertness, and watchfulness
always guard every door of the senses.*

We should post recollection, alertness, and watchfulness as guards at the gateways of our body, speech, and mind and have them restrain us from committing unwholesome actions through these three doors. To safeguard the treasure of realizations stored within us, we should lock these doors from both inside and out.

We can liken the mental faculty of recollection, or mindfulness, to an iron hook. When the mind wanders to nonvirtue, recollection hooks it and brings it back to a wholesome position.

Three times during the day and night, again and again,
investigate your mental continuum.

At all times we must analyze our stream of thoughts to see
whether the actions we are doing will benefit our future lives or
if they are just for momentary pleasure.

Proclaim your own faults and seek not mistakes in others.

To hide our shortcomings and harbor them inside only
increases our guilt and discomfort. It is far better to reveal them
to others: this lessens their effect. It is especially important
to do so when generating the awakening mind. However, we
should be discreet and careful with regard to whom we give
such information since it may easily be misunderstood or
misrepresented.

On the other hand, we should not be constantly on the look-
out for faults in others. If we see their mistakes but never our
own, we are like a mirror, which reflects only what is outside
it but never itself. The faults we criticize in others are only our
own projected onto them; if they were not, they would not
bother us, and we would not even notice them. Furthermore,
we should realize that whatever flaws appear to stand out in
others are perceptions no different from our usual mistaken
view of all things as truly independent. The faults we see are,
in fact, dependent on many circumstances, such as the person's
previous actions and emotional afflictions and our view of the
situation. We cannot find a truly independent and substan-
tially existing possessor of shortcomings. By looking at things
in this way, we can use this opportunity to make an ultimate
analysis of the situation and reflect on the emptiness of our
own projections.

13

Hide your own good qualities but
proclaim the good qualities of others.

There is no need to boast about our own knowledge and accomplishments. Tsongkhapa has said, "Your own attainments and insight should be like a butter lamp burning inside a vase: it illuminates the interior but is not displayed outwardly."

It is especially important never to boast about or exhibit extraphysical powers such as heightened awareness or clairvoyance. To demonstrate them with an impure motive serves no beneficial purpose. Dromtönpa, Atisha's closest Tibetan disciple, said, "If you can see your own faults and never look for those of others, then even though you may have no other good qualities, you are very wise."

Therefore, not seeking faults in others is in itself a very great Dharma practice. Dromtönpa and others like him were all very humble although they had great spiritual attainments. Atisha has also said, "My compassion is due to the kindness of my teachers of the awakening mind; my realization of emptiness is due to the kindness of my teacher of emptiness. Nothing is my own."

Once, Dromtönpa was requested to give his biography and an initiation but refused out of humility. Pressed by Atisha, he finally consented and gave the empowerment of one of the most complicated practices, the Sixteen Essences of the Kadam, which has sixteen mandalas within one another. With a similar lack of pride we each should keep quiet about our attainments and good qualities yet make known the excellences of others. However, be careful that your praise does not simply arouse others' pride in themselves.

Dwelling on the flaws of others is a vain attempt to hide our own. When our conversation is only the criticism of others, the person to whom we are speaking tends not to listen and forms a poor impression of us. Thus, to speak in this manner produces the opposite of our purpose of protecting our ego and making others like us; others will speak as poorly of us as we do of them. This is the law of cause and effect—that our actions bring about like results.

Reject acquisitions and honors and always reject desire for fame.

If in approaching spiritual teachings we give up all desire for respect, fame, reputation, and personal gain, then whatever we study and practice will be beneficial. However, should we have studied two hundred volumes only for intellectual stimulation and gain, they will never be of ultimate benefit to us. The assimilation of two pages of essential instructions with pure motivation is more valuable than years of studying texts for selfish reasons.

Desire little, be content, and repay acts of kindness.

Full contentment with what we have will bring us peace of mind, whether we practice Dharma or not. If we are satisfied with what we have, we shall not strive to acquire superfluous objects and shall avoid suffering both the hardships involved in trying to obtain things and the frustration of being unable to acquire them. Having little desire and being content go together. Without these two inner qualities we become competitive. In his *Friendly Letter,* Nagarjuna said,

> If you have contentment, then even though you may
> be robbed of everything, consider yourself the richest
> man; but should you lack contentment, then no matter
> how rich you may be, you are a servant of your wealth.

15

If we have no contentment, we can never live like Milarepa on nettles in a cave. He said, "For salt, I use nettles; for spice, now I add in nettles."

At the time of Buddha Shakyamuni there lived a merchant who returned to his homeland, bringing an extremely rare and valuable object with the intention of giving it to the poorest person there. When he arrived, he gave it to the king! He explained that this was because, even though the king was the richest in material possessions, he was the poorest in his mind since he lacked contentment. It makes no sense to become extravagantly rich because we cannot wear double or triple clothes or eat ten times the normal amount of food. Both kings and beggars can only eat and drink enough to satisfy their hunger and thirst, and they require merely sufficient clothing to protect their bodies from the elements.

Atisha further mentions that we should always remember the kindness others have shown us and return it when they are in need. To accept the kindness and favors of another and then later be indifferent when that same person is in need is extremely callous. Buddha Shakyamuni said in a sutra:

> Those sentient beings who, after becoming rich through
> receiving help from others ignore those who helped
> them when they were poor—they are worse than
> animals. Even dogs gratefully acknowledge those who
> have given them food.

Meditate on love and compassion and stabilize the awakening mind.

We should combine wishing to repay the kindness that others have shown us with meditating on pure love for them. To develop a loving heart is very important for our own happiness. We cannot expect friendliness from others if we, in turn, are not appreciative of them. These are totally interdependent. Nagarjuna has emphasized that meditating on pure love and giving love to others is better than giving them material comforts; it gives more lasting pleasure. Buddha Shakyamuni has said in many discourses that even one instant of pure love or benevolence is better than giving something tangible. This does not mean that we should not be generous, but rather that the results of pure love are more powerful than giving material objects. Pure love is the intense wish that all beings be happy.

Because compassion is the essence of Dharma, meditation on compassion was also greatly emphasized by Buddha Shakyamuni. If we pick up the handle, we pick up the pot. Similarly, if we meditate on and develop compassion—the wish that all others be without suffering—we hold within us the essence of all other Dharma practices.

We confirm and stabilize the awakening mind by means of love and compassion. This mind continues to develop until it is completely pure and the consummate fulfillment of buddhahood is reached. Atisha urges us to stabilize the awakening mind because, even though we may meditate on love and compassion for others, we may become discouraged when we are treated maliciously. We may think, "With people like this how can I possibly maintain the altruistic aspiration to gain complete realization for the sake of all others, including them?" Because discouragement only weakens the awakening mind, we should not allow ourselves to be affected by what others say or do, no matter how cruel it may be.

Shariputra, one of the main disciples of Buddha Shakyamuni, did not have the Mahayana motivation to liberate all beings, but it is said that he almost developed the awakening mind. However, just as he was about to stabilize it, a man who was actually a malevolent being, a *mara*, approached him and demanded that he cut off his right hand and give it to him. This Shariputra did and offered it to the man with his left hand. However, because presenting anything with the left hand is highly improper according to Indian custom, the man refused to accept it. He said, "You should present me your right hand with your right hand." At this, Shariputra became completely discouraged and thought, "If there are such evil beings as this, how can I ever work for their benefit and develop bodhichitta?" Thus he reverted back to the lesser motivation of the Hinayana, working to gain liberation from cyclic existence for himself alone. While we are trying to generate the pure awakening mind, we should always expect to meet such difficult people; then they will never overwhelm us. If we naively expect everyone else to be pleasant, we shall only be disappointed.

Dignaga, one of the great Indian logicians, was once meditating in a cave, preparing to write a text on logic. After composing the first pages, he left his cave for a moment. While he was gone, an opponent came and erased the work he had done. This happened again, and on the third occasion Dignaga left a note saying, "Such action is pointless. If you want to oppose me, come and debate openly." The opponent did this and lost. He was so angry that through his miraculous powers, he produced fire from his mouth and, out of spite, burned everything in the cave. Dignaga became so disheartened that he said, "If there are such people as this who do not even accept logic, I shall throw my writing slate up into the air; if it falls down again, I shall give up working for others." He threw the slate up, but it did not fall back. He looked up and saw Manjushri holding it. Manjushri said to him, "My spiritual son, you are about to make a grave mistake." With such encouragement Dignaga maintained his awakening mind and composed the *Pramanasamuccaya*, or *The Compendium of Valid Reasoning*.

Just as great beings like Shariputra and Dignaga were faced with such problems, we too must expect similar obstacles to our development. Adverse circumstances test our courage, our strength of mind, and the depth of our conviction in the Dharma. There is nothing exceptional about practicing Dharma in a good environment and atmosphere. The true test is if we can maintain our practice in adverse conditions.

Avoid the ten unwholesome actions and always stabilize your faith.

We should guard our ethical discipline. Not letting it disintegrate, we should maintain the integrity of our actions through our body, speech, and mind. The ten unwholesome actions are killing, stealing, adultery, lying, slandering, speaking divisively, talking pointlessly, covetousness, maliciousness, and holding such wrong views as disbelief in buddhahood and in the law of actions and their consequences.

This is because it is a fundamental tenet of Buddhism that wholesome actions will result in a happy and beneficial rebirth and vice-versa. Thus it is said that the whole practice of ethics is based on understanding that future results will arise from present actions. Dharma practice is not what we do outwardly, like remaining in a room and chanting, but depends on whether we observe carefully and with full awareness the law of cause and effect, even if we do no formal meditation.

Furthermore, Atisha advises us to stabilize our faith and confidence. In the Buddhist context, faith does not arise from fear, but is based on reason. Confidence in the teachings arises when we experience for ourselves how nondeceptive they are. It is said that such conviction is the mother of firm understanding.

Conquer anger and arrogance and possess a humble mind.

Anger and arrogance are the worst of all psychological afflictions. Anger is more serious than the worst attachment because although the latter is unwholesome, by its nature it does not necessarily affect others adversely. Anger, on the other hand, directly and negatively affects not only the one who is angry but others as well. To have anger and arrogance reduces the force of the awakening mind considerably.

People with strong conceit imagine themselves to be superior and thus never heed the advice of others. Never listening, they never assimilate anything. Since they feel they are so knowledgeable, they must always defend their own position. Just as a high plateau is the last area to turn green with grass in the summer, a proud person will be the last to really know anything.

The person who has at least conquered anger and pride, and is humble in all actions, will everywhere be happy and accepted by others.

Avoid wrong livelihoods and live a life of truth.

We should not rob, steal, or acquire our living by any means that are deceitful. Even merely eating food that others have gained by wrong methods is an obstacle to insight. There are five wrong livelihoods: flattery, pressuring someone into giving us something by saying that this is what was done previously, obtaining something by telling someone it is a penalty for an imaginary offense, bribery, and deceit. To live on what has been stolen is an especially unjustified means of existence; living in this way causes harm to others because we consume what is rightfully theirs. However, when we refuse to accept stolen articles, we should do so without offending the other person's feelings. Even if a person is desperate and poor, it is better for that person to beg than to steal in order to live, because the consequence of stealing is increased poverty. If you are the one who has to beg, then accept with gratitude whatever you are given.

Luipa, one of the Indian *mahasiddhas*,[1] was very poor and went to the banks of the river Ganges to obtain food. He noticed that the fishermen left behind the fish entrails, so he thought, "Since no one owns them, these would be the best to eat." He lived in this way and through tantric practices obtained the full realization of Heruka[2] in his very lifetime.

Abandon all worldly possessions and be adorned by the gems of superiors.

Atisha does not imply that we should literally discard all our possessions. Rather, we should renounce and not feel great attachment to those things that in the first place are difficult to obtain and, once obtained, are difficult to protect, involve the danger of being lost, and may cost us our life should we try to preserve them. Our possessions should not arouse feelings of miserliness in us, nor cause us concern if they are lost.

It is inappropriate to be miserly about a religious object since we should not regard it as part of our wealth. If we simply regard it as symbolic of our refuge and, through our veneration for it, as a source of merit, we shall not be concerned by its loss. A true religious object should be considered priceless, but not for its monetary value.

Thus we should abandon attachment for external ornaments while retaining within us the gems of a superior person. There are seven of these inner gems to adorn our mind, named and explained at the conclusion of this text.

Abandon all frivolities and abide in solitude.

This does not necessarily imply that we should be fanatical and live completely alone in a cave. Yet we should not regularly

21

waste time in frivolous activities or seek diversions in irrelevant gatherings. Such pastimes serve only to reduce the intensity of our practice. One great lama in Lhasa gave the following advice to those who had come from the outer provinces of Tibet to hear a discourse:

> Do not meet each other too regularly, but gather together only once in a while, otherwise you defeat the purpose of having come here. If you really wish to meet and have parties all the time, why do you not go home?

This advice applies to anyone who sincerely wishes to study and practice Dharma. To meet others occasionally is necessary to refresh our understanding, but to do so too often is a distraction. Whenever two or more people meet, it is inevitable that there will be idle gossip and talk that may arouse anger or attachment. A great meditator once said,

> As a beginner I find this life in the mountains enjoyable. Birds and animals come to visit me, and I can freely talk with them without it giving rise to anger, attachment, and a host of other delusions.

Abandon all senseless talk and always control your speech.

The result of idle gossip and unnecessary talk is time wasted. Such pastimes are indeed relaxing and enjoyable and are often carried on until the small hours of the morning; yet were we to spend that time meditating, we would be snoring long before midnight! The Junior Tutor to His Holiness the Dalai Lama, the late Trijang Rinpoche, said,

> If you find your mind in a state not conducive to performing virtuous actions, do not go and talk idly with someone. Instead, go to sleep. You might not

accumulate much virtue but at least you will not accumulate nonvirtue. The indifferent state of sleep is much more relaxing than idle talk with friends.

The great Nyingma *dzogchen*[3] master, Patrul Rinpoche, said,

> Now that I am ready to go into retreat, I shall stop talking altogether. I shall cease sending my mind out to seek the faults in others, and instead I shall spend my time looking within. Life is too short to waste in mental wandering and limitless gossip.

When seeing your master or teacher, perform services with respect.

When we meet and see our own teachers, we should always act respectfully and assist them by whatever means we can.

Toward a person having the eye of the doctrine and toward sentient beings who are beginners develop the recognition of them as teachers.

23

We should regard as our teacher both those who have insight into the meaning of the Dharma and those who are just beginning to practice. We should rejoice in any accomplishment of someone following the Dharma, whether the person is advanced or a mere beginner.

Abandon misleading friends and rely on virtuous spiritual companions.

Buddha Shakyamuni said in one of his discourses,

> Fear not a rogue elephant, but have fear of misleading friends, who can destroy both your body and your mind.

Misleading companions may not appear as obvious threats to our quest for inner happiness, but since they may divert our energy, we should not cultivate such friendships. The Kadam Geshe Potowa said,

> Misleading friends do not have horns on their heads or
> wear black cloaks, but they throw you
> further into samsara.

In this sense even parents may sometimes be misleading and, if this is so, we must avoid their adverse influence. If we are always in the company of misleading friends, then, like the coal miner whose face and hands are blackened by his actions, we shall be influenced by their negativities. Associating with people whose actions are wholesome is like whitewashing a wall: we become covered in the whiteness of their virtue.

Much of our personal development depends on the influence of our friends. If they set a bad example, then in our present state of weakness their influence can adversely affect our behavior and state of mind. Hence, we must temporarily avoid negative friends. Only when our practice has strength and stability can such people benefit us, and we them. One Nyingma lama said,

> If you live with someone who is generous, you too
> become generous; if you live with someone who has
> strong ethics, you also become an ethical person.
> However, if you are with someone of disreputable
> character, you will become lax, and your whole practice
> will degenerate.

When we are with spiritual companions, we remain conscious of our motives and feel a desire to improve ourselves and follow their example. Bodhisattvas who are very firm in their practice are virtuous friends to everyone and cannot be influenced by unwholesome company; with the strength of their realization they transcend distinctions of good and bad, yet their actions are spontaneously positive.

If we find companions an annoyance and a hindrance, we should not necessarily disregard them; the problem may be within us. Buddha Shakyamuni said, "Judge not others; judge only yourself."

What appear to be faults in others may actually be reflections of our own emotional afflictions.

Abandon minds of anger and unhappiness, and wherever you go be happy.

If we are angry and aggressive, happiness will always elude us. Happiness and contentment are dependent entirely on our attitudes toward daily situations and life in general. Full of anger and aggression, we cannot even enjoy the good fortune of wealth or delicious food, yet with peace of mind we shall be content with the most basic diet and simple dwellings. To carry a burden of heavy attachments and commitments will always be a disturbance; even our dreams will be uneasy. A true practitioner of Dharma should be like a bee that is never attracted to just one flower, but flies from one to another. Unlike most people who are fastidious and critical, a spiritual person should have no preferences. To insist upon specific foods or to be dependent upon luxuries is only a further commitment to ego-centered preferences and, as such, is an unnecessary discipline. We should be able to adapt to whatever circumstances we find.

By remaining in one place too long we make friends, as well as enemies, and soon we become attached to the familiarity of our environment. Tsongkhapa was called "The Wanderer" because as soon as people heard that he was in one place and came to him presenting offerings, he would move on. He acted in this way until he achieved full realization. After that he remained in one place and, speaking from his own experience, gave discourses, founded monasteries, and performed other beneficial activities.

25

Abandon attachment to everything and abide free from attachment.

If we feel strongly attached to an object, we should give it away, sell it, or at least put it out of sight. In this way we shall lessen our attachment. For people who wish to meditate intensively, it is recommended that they abandon gross sensory stimuli. Thus, one should live in a simple but pleasant room; it should not be elaborate. For this reason caves are more suitable for deep meditation. They are not places that have been made attractive by human effort, and a meditator will develop less attachment for rocks and earth than for a comfortable room.

A great Tibetan meditator, Togme Zangpo, who composed the *Thirty-Seven Practices of Bodhisattvas*,[4] went to live in a cave in his late twenties and remained there until he was sixty, making friends with birds and animals. He said,

> For me to go into a cave for meditation is very
> useful. If I look above, there are no authorities or
> relatives; if I look below, there are no servants.
> I am left alone with my mind, without worldly
> distractions or extraneous activities.

We should realize that we must utilize our mind and do something constructive with it. If we are continually distracted in divisive activities, we shall never gain insight into the true nature of reality.

Attachment will never procure you a happy rebirth;
it kills the life of liberation.

Atisha is very emphatic about abandoning attachment because not only can it deprive us of happiness in this life, it can also deny us the opportunity of a better rebirth, liberation from cyclic existence, or freedom of mind. As the opponent to the attachments of lust and passion, we should have strong ethics.

Wherever you see practices leading to happiness,
always exert effort in them.

Whatever activities we do should be weighed on the scale of our intelligence to determine whether or not the outcome will be beneficial. If an action will yield only confusion and dissatisfaction for ourselves and others, do not perform it. When acting impetuously, we forget to take into consideration the consequences of our actions. Elderly people are often looked upon as conservative, since they tend to consider a variety of possibilities before they act, and then do things slowly.

Human beings are endowed with a fundamental intelligence that if utilized wisely can bring everlasting peace and happiness. If we neglect to use it, we have defeated the purpose of having achieved such a precious incarnation. To act only for the pleasure of this life, without consideration for others, is to behave no better than an animal and is not in keeping with our human potential.

We should also think earnestly before taking vows or making spiritual commitments. Shantideva, in the *Guide to a Bodhisattva's Way of Life*, says,

Do not take vows in haste. Consider first if you can
keep them. If you can, then let them remain unbroken;
keep your vows steadily.

Whatever you have started to do, accomplish that very thing first.
Do everything well in this way, otherwise nothing will be achieved.

There are too many things in this world to be learned, and life is too short to learn everything, so we should complete that which we have begun rather than dabbling in many things. It is best to find one thing that is suited to our taste and then taste it fully. In following spiritual practices, if we act like a dilettante, always tasting a little of many things, such as trying out many personal deities and the meditation practices of many different traditions, we shall never be able to accomplish any of them. Also, if we sample many religions, picking up a bit of Hinduism, Buddhism, Christianity, Islam, or whatever, we shall only be left with confusion. Since we cannot know everything and become an all-knowing master of samsara, it is better to learn one thing and learn it thoroughly.

For instance, some students try to learn many languages but often end up not knowing even one well. If they were to learn one language well, they would be able to delve into many aspects of the culture and religion associated with it. Not to learn one thing thoroughly is like trying to sew with a needle pointed at both ends: we shall never be able to make any progress. Doing too many things divides our attention and disperses single-pointedness. Some monks in Tibet would come to a monastery and first do a short retreat, then leave and return again later to study another subject, only to end up without any realizations whatsoever.

If there were two masons building two walls, and one built up layer after layer steadily while the other worked in sporadic bursts, the latter would never complete the task. We should, therefore, be like the first mason and build the walls of our spiritual mansion by working steadily all the time. We should always make allowances for things to take time and should not expect realization or "instant bliss" to follow from practices of a few weeks, months, or even a year. Insight and increased awareness in every life situation can only come about over several years. In fact, if we have begun generating the awakening mind, for instance, we should set as our aim the intention to maintain it over the whole of this present lifetime as well as throughout all future lives. If we extend the scope of our vision beyond the limited context of this one life and begin to view things in a far greater perspective, it is certain that we shall develop insight in accordance with our efforts. Even if we do not fully develop the awakening mind, because of its altruistic and all-pervasive frame of reference, we shall certainly become a kinder human being.

Always be apart from liking evil.

We should reject the pleasures that stem from wrong actions since the enjoyment derived from indulging in emotional afflictions soon leads to pain. Letting ourselves be blown about by the winds of our negativities indicates that we have a completely misguided approach to life. Instead, we should savor the lasting delight that arises from skillful behavior and meditation.

Whenever a pompous mind arises, flatten such arrogance.
Recall the teachings of your master.

Pride, or conceit, is one of the worst emotional afflictions. If we feel that by having developed the awakening mind we are superior to others, then everyone will disparage us. If we are supercilious and pompous, no one will find us compatible. As an opponent to arrogance we should meditate on impermanence and death.

Very few people have a steady or stable experience of life. For most, their emotions ebb and flow like the tides. Sometimes we may feel proud of signs of accomplishment, and yet at other times we may be depressed when our defilements and

29

habitual propensities overwhelm us. All such feelings are relative to one another because discouragement exists only in relation to elation; neither one is independent. It is beneficial if our life flows with little major change, like a wide river. Therefore, we should not become too excited when we accomplish a great deal, or depressed when we fail to do so. If we feel self-pity, we should contemplate on our good fortune at having a fully endowed precious human form.

When a cowardly mind arises, praise the sublimity of the mind.

We should try to develop the courage of a warrior and the strength of mind to exert enthusiastic effort in the practices. If we are not brave in our approach, we shall become bored with meditation. If a bucket can be filled by drops of water, why cannot the mind be liberated by progressive inner development? If the mind can be directed onto the correct path, then since it does not have a static existence, it is certainly capable of gaining complete release from confusion. This potential to become fully awakened is the sublime nature of the mind itself.

Whenever objects of attraction or aversion arise, meditate on the emptiness of both; view them as illusions and emanations.

If we develop strong attachment or aggression toward anyone or anything, it is especially effective to regard them as we would regard dreams, illusions, or emanations. A dream arises and passes, yet has no substantial existence, like a hallucination or an illusion. Anything that causes emotional defilements to arise should likewise be seen as illusory.

When hearing any offensive words, view them as an echo.

Whenever we hear discordant and abusive words that we do not like, we should regard them as the echo of a sound we ourselves

have made. Unpleasant sounds are echoes of our own unpleas-
antness, and praises are echoes of pleasing sounds we have
uttered.

When your body is afflicted by harm, view this as your previous actions.

It is a skillful practice to blame all that goes wrong and any
injury or harm that comes to us as the ripening of our past
unskillful actions. We should think that we have committed
worse actions in the past and that our present difficulties
stem from this. To do so quickly ends any internal conflict.
Accumulation of unwholesome acts leads to our own suffering.
We do not have to lift up a pick and shovel and work hard to
collect negative actions and troubles; we can do so quietly just
by generating dark thoughts. It is not true that our problems
come from outside us; all are created by ourselves. If we search
inwardly, we can reach a lasting state of happiness, but to look
outwardly for the cause of confusion and frustration will never
uncover the solution.

Abide well in solitude, beyond town limits, like the corpses of wild game.

Since we should dedicate all our efforts in the beginning stages
of practice toward self-observation and taming and pacifying
the mind, it is beneficial to live in solitude. The more distrac-
tions there are outside, the more there will be inside. The quieter
it is outside, the quieter the mind will become. Therefore,
Atisha suggests that we hide like the corpses of wild game. For
instance, cats do not generally die in their master's home, but
leave and die alone. In a similar fashion, we should retreat to
places of isolation in order to engage in intensive meditation.
This requires strength and courage in addition to enthusiastic
effort. Milarepa has said,

31

If my relatives do not hear of my happiness, my enemies do not learn of my suffering, and I die alone
without any mourners, then all my wishes as a yogi will
have been fulfilled.

In mentioning the optimum circumstances for serious meditation, it is not expected that everyone must do the same when
following Buddhist teachings. It shows us how great masters of
the past have engaged in such practices and succeeded in gaining
full realization. To bear such things in mind can give us further courage and perhaps a few people may be prepared to gain
ultimate benefit for themselves and others through undertaking
such practices.

Be by yourself, conceal yourself, and dwell without attachment.

When we go into retreat, it is best to be alone in places where
great meditators of the past have meditated; the blessings of the
location can assist our practice greatly. Bodh Gaya, for instance,
the most sacred place in the Buddhist world, is said to be the
place where all buddhas have attained and will attain full awakening. The power of such a place is so strong that even a worldly
person who goes there develops spiritual feelings and is moti-
vated to circumambulate the temple and contemplate. Visiting
such a place reconfirms our motivation again and again.

Always stabilize awareness of your yidam and,
whenever laziness or lassitude arise, enumerate these faults
to yourself and feel remorse from your heart.

To stabilize our personal deity, or yidam, means that we should
always confirm the motivation for our actions and bear in mind
the goal of complete union with the fully awakened state our
yidam symbolizes. It is stated in the *Ten Innermost Jewels of the Kadam*

Tradition that we should always send forth the diamond-hard conviction of a pure motivation before any action. With this as a basis, nothing can alter our meditation plans or intentions.

Then, when an opponent to meditation arises, such as laziness, lassitude, or mental wandering, we shall quickly be able to return to the object of our meditation by recollecting our motivation. We should follow the example of Kadam Geshe Bangung Gyal who, when he found himself getting lazy, would say to himself, "If you do not watch out, I am going to tell everyone exactly what you are doing and expose you in a disgraceful way." We should follow our inner teacher and correct our own faults. This inner discipline and regret at mistakes is the essence of the practice.

If you see others, speak calmly and sincerely.

We should not be restless in our behavior, but should be calm and act with deliberation. We should not be conceited in our actions like some people who, when asked for directions, just rudely gesture in a vague and unhelpful manner. Instead of being arrogant like this, we should reply sincerely to any questions we may be asked. Being conceited is only a means of bolstering the ego's grasping for a false sense of security. Such behavior definitely elicits negative feelings about us in others. Self-centered people do not want to be bothered to go out of their way to help anyone; even if they know how to help, they may say the opposite just to be malicious.

Avoid a wrathful and frowning expression and always remain cheerful.

When we are asked to do something, we should not wrinkle our face in indignation like an old hag, but should accept whatever it may be cheerfully. This advice is very useful for a salesman or dealer: if he is always smiling, he will attract customers; if he is always sour-faced, no one will ever buy from him. However, there was one Kadam geshe, Langri Tangpa, who had such an unpleasant expression that he was nicknamed "Dark Face." Once his disciples asked him to smile because people were talking detrimentally about him. He replied,

> I have no time to smile in this state of cyclic existence.
> The more I think of its miserable nature, the more
> sober I become!

When seeing others, continuously be pleased to give without being miserly.

When living constantly with others, we should not be possessive with our belongings. Instead, we should be open-handed and should avoid developing the strong attachment of thinking, "This is mine."

Discard all jealousy.

Envy, or jealousy, is another major hindrance to happiness. If we are jealous of others, we shall always be in a state of emotional instability. Should others succeed in their work, the resentment we feel from our envy will never affect them; it only causes unnecessary misery in us. The opponent for envious thoughts is rejoicing in the accomplishments of others.

To protect the mind of another, avoid all conflict and always have patience.

If we consider ourselves true followers of Buddhist teachings, we should try hard to avoid causing conflict in the minds of others by never arguing or violently disagreeing with what they say. For instance, it is pointless to argue over such topics as which nation has more political power and is more advanced. Most people stubbornly hold on to their views in these matters, and such differences of opinion can never be resolved. If we are involved in this type of discussion, it is best to agree with what the other says since this will be most pleasing. If we disagree, contradict, and dispute what others say, it senselessly hurts their feelings and leaves them upset for many hours. We should be able to endure others' words, for without the strength of patience, it is barely possible to practice Dharma.

Do not be fickle or a flatterer, but always be capable of remaining steadfast.

We should never be two-faced, acting pleasantly to someone while in their presence, only to show a different face when they are gone. Do not be hypocritical, appearing to like someone while inwardly harboring dislike. Furthermore, we should not be fickle with people, making friends easily and then rejecting them just as quickly. If we make friends, we should maintain that friendship for a long time. We should not make a new friend, only to see that the person has faults like everyone else, and after a month disparage him or her in front of others. To behave like this is an obvious sign that we are uncertain of ourselves and lack any inner conviction or stability.

Avoid belittling others and remain respectful in your manners.

We should never be contemptuous of people who are lower in social or economic position, or who are racially different from us; instead, we should treat everyone with respect. Some people make friends only with those who are rich and influential. If later such friends are ignored when they have somehow fallen to a lower status, this is an extremely callous action. It is wrong to be proud and remove ourselves from others who are not as well off as we. This is not to say that we should avoid those who are wealthy and socially prominent, but we should be respectful of everyone and treat all equally without classifying people into preferential groups.

When giving advice to others,
have compassion and thoughts for their benefit.

When we help others by giving them advice or instructions, we should do so out of compassion and never for monetary gain, fame, respect, or some misguided sense of self-righteous duty. A teacher with feelings of love and compassion for the students has a far greater degree of communication. Without these qualities, the teacher will never be able to bridge the gap of skepticism.

Do not disparage spiritual doctrines
and be intent on whichever you admire.

We should follow a spiritual system that suits our own abilities best and avoid criticizing other traditions. People with different dispositions naturally follow different traditions. It is not up to us, just because we follow one system, to discourage others from the path they have chosen and criticize them, discrediting their choice. In speaking disparagingly about other religious systems, we commit the serious nonvirtue of abandoning Dharma. Buddha Shakyamuni said,

> The consequences of religious sectarianism are far worse than killing saints or destroying as many religious monuments as there are grains of sand in the River Ganges.

Through the door of the ten Dharma practices,
exert effort throughout both day and night.

As bodhisattvas, we should intensively follow the practices of the ten transcendent perfections. The first six are the commonly known ones of generosity, ethical discipline, patience, enthusiastic effort, meditative stability, and intelligent awareness. The four additional ones are of strength, prayers of aspiration for the path, skillful means, and primordial awareness. Buddha Shakyamuni said that we should follow these ten Dharma practices sincerely.

The aforementioned list is for those who are following practices of the Great Vehicle, the Mahayana. For those who do not engage actively in this path, there is another set of ten general practices explained by Maitreya, the coming buddha. They are known as the ten daily practices: (1) copying and writing out scriptures, (2) making offerings to the Three Supreme Jewels, (3) giving generously to the poor and sick, (4) listening to discourses on Dharma, (5) reading scriptures to oneself and others, (6) taking to heart the essence of the teachings through meditation, (7) explaining the meaning of the Dharma, (8) reciting the *Heart Sutra* or any of Buddha's sutras, (9) contemplating the meaning of the texts, and (10) meditating single-pointedly on the meaning of the teachings.

Thus we should perform the ten transcendent perfections or the ten daily practices, thereby pointing all our actions in a skillful direction. In this regard it is often recommended that we sleep as little as possible. Buddha Shakyamuni has said that sleep between the hours just before and after midnight is most beneficial. We should wake in the early hours of the morning and continue our meditation. Even today there are many practitioners who practice so intensively that they do not leave their meditation mats even to sleep.

Past meditators and Dharma masters have found the early hours of the morning most conducive to meditative clarity, but this is a habit that should be built up gradually. When we begin, we will find sleep more inviting than meditation. A deeper realization of the preciousness of a human form endowed with intelligence will impel us to pursue practice more vigorously. A few people, by the time they reach their twenties and early thirties have already devoted their lives fully to practice, but most of us never even remember how we wasted the early years, how we lost that time. It is to propel us into meditation that recollection of impermanence is stressed. If we begin with a good foundation, there will be enough strength in our activities to enable us to engage in the intensive meditations of tantra. Without this basis, even the practice of Guhyasamaja, the "king of tantras," will be ineffectual.

> *Whatever virtues are collected during the three times,*
> *dedicate them for the unsurpassable great awakening.*
> *Distribute your merit for all sentient beings.*

To dedicate the skillful actions we do toward our own and all sentient beings' attainment of buddhahood is like asking someone to keep these actions safe for us. If we fail to direct them toward this highest aim, the merit will ripen only as a mundane benefit or, unfortunately, may easily be destroyed by anger and the like.

> *Always offer the seven-limbed prayer and great aspirations for the path.*

Every day we should perform the preliminary practice known as the seven-limbed prayer, symbolized by the seven water-bowl offerings on an altar. All sentient beings possess within themselves the buddha-nature that, although covered by the veil of conflicting emotions and ignorance, can be revealed through means such as those contained in the seven-limbed prayer.

Prostrations, the first of the seven limbs, is usually coupled with taking refuge in the Three Supreme Jewels. In prostrating it is essential to keep the mind on our motivation, not allowing it to dwell on the physical act or the process of counting. We may make half prostrations—touching the knees, hands, and forehead to the ground—or full ones with our body fully extended. We should rise immediately, thinking that this is symbolic of rising quickly out of worldly confusion and misery. Prostration is one of the strongest opponent forces for pride since it is a form of surrendering—a practice greatly emphasized by Atisha. In the context of the extraordinary preliminary practices, this is especially effective for cleansing obstacles and accumulating merit. Based on instructions from our own teacher, we can recite the refuge formula or a text such as the *Confession Sutra*[5] while performing these prostrations.

The second limb is making offerings, a powerful opponent for miserliness. Although there are specific offerings that can be made, they can include anything beautiful, such as pure water, flowers, candles, incense, sweets, fruit, and perfume—provided that they are chosen without thought for the eight worldly concerns.[6] To make offerings to a visualized assembly representing the objects of refuge plants a seed that will ripen into transcendent benefits for us.

Confession, the third limb of the prayer, is an opponent to all three source-afflictions: aggression, attachment, and ignorance. The practice is performed by means of the four opponent forces. First, we should apply the opponent of strong regret at having committed wrong actions, feeling as though we had taken poison. We should then vow not to repeat such an unskillful action, just as a person who had taken poison would vow never to do so again. Third, we should go sincerely for refuge and generate the awakening mind. Since we usually commit unwholesome actions against either the objects of refuge or other sentient beings, going for refuge purifies the former and generating the awakening mind the latter. Finally, we should apply the force of countermeasures, such as prostrations or Vajrasattva meditation, which will purify us of the instincts of unskillful actions.

Rejoicing is the fourth aspect of the prayer, and it means being joyful about our own virtuous actions and those of others. Rejoicing in others' deeds is the opponent force for jealousy. It is said that from sincerely rejoicing, we shall have a pleasing appearance in our future birth. This is one of the reasons why the faces of saints and enlightened beings are so pleasing to look at: they have rejoiced very much in others' virtuous acts, and they also radiate compassion.

The fifth is to request the awakened beings to continue turning the wheel of the doctrine and giving teachings. This stimulates our insight because it is by hearing the Dharma that we develop inner weapons to cut through our lack of awareness of the true nature of reality. Just as we need matches to light a lamp, so do we need the guidance of a spiritual master to ignite the flame of wisdom within us. These actions counter the unskillful deeds of holding on to wrong views and being bigoted in our outlook.

The sixth limb is requesting the fully-awakened beings to live long lives and not to pass away. This eliminates unskillful acts against our spiritual teachers, such as not following their instructions, and results in an increase of our own lifespan. Hence, this practice is called the Nectar of Immortality.

Finally, we should dedicate any merit we have gained toward our own attainment of buddhahood and the release from suffering of all living beings.

After this, we should also offer prayers of aspiration for the path, such as wishing to be reborn in a position of influence and thereby be able to benefit many more beings. This is like the desire to be born as a "religious king," a leader who always weighs the affairs of state in terms of the law of actions and their fruit for the benefit of the majority.

If you act in this way, the two accumulations of
merit and wisdom will be accomplished.

"Accumulations" refers to the mass of virtuous positive energy that supports us in our practice. The accumulation of physical merit through practices such as generosity acts as the cause for attaining the perfect body of form, or *rupakaya*, of an awakened being. The accumulation of "wisdom" is gained by understanding the emptiness of all things and acts as the seed for gaining the insight of an awakened being, known as the perfect body of truth, or *dharmakaya*.

Also, with the eradication of the two obscurations,
thus fulfilling the purpose of having gained a human form,
unsurpassable full awakening will be achieved.

The way in which we attain ultimate realization is by clearing away the two obscurations that prevent insight into the true nature of reality. These are the obscuration of emotional afflictions and the obscuration to the knowledge of everything. The former prevents freedom from the forces of cyclic existence, the latter prevents the omniscience of buddhahood. We begin actually to eliminate them only when we have advanced well into the practice.

If we do not at least try to lessen the force of emotional afflictions, the grosser of these two obscurations, we may not experience happiness and peace of mind even if all the external circumstances for material well-being are present. Although we have now reached the moon—a goal long desired by many—universal happiness has not been achieved. In order to make this life truly meaningful, we must work inwardly. If we are not able to eliminate even one single emotional affliction during our lifetime, then we have been born only to give suffering to our mother, and in this respect we are no different from animals.

Most intelligent people recognize that they are constantly under the sway of various emotions often leading to psychological conflict. If we are intent on following a spiritual path but do not try to reduce these obstructions, our approach is basically superficial. However, we cannot become enlightened in one day. Our mind is like an onion, and each day and month of practice progressively peels away the layers of delusion. Finally, one day we reach the insubstantial essence and are fully aware of our true nature. This attainment of complete realization depends on no one other than ourselves. One Tibetan master of meditation said,

> We should differentiate right from wrong on our own
> and should not regard surrendering to our spiritual
> master as a total dependence on him like a baby
> sucking the breast of its mother. Our approach must
> involve the realization that the development of intuitive
> awareness depends on our own efforts and intelligence.

Fundamentally, to practice Dharma means to integrate the essence of the teachings into our daily life by trying to make others, as well as ourselves, happy. If we fail to do this, then even receiving teachings through visionary states of mind would be meaningless, since the words and teachings are nothing but a means to change our attitude.

The gem of faith, the gem of ethics, the gem of generosity,
the gem of hearing, the gem of consideration, the gem of shame,
and the gem of intelligence: these are the seven supreme gems.
These seven gems are never exhausted.
Do not tell this to nonhumans.

Even though we cannot wear all our outer ornaments at once, we can adorn our mind with all seven inner ornaments of the *arya's* gems. The gem of faith is certain conviction in the non-deceptive nature of the objects of refuge. The gem of ethical discipline leads us to follow the outer and inner modes of proper behavior.

If we lack the gem of generosity, we shall be miserly and mentally poor even if we have great wealth. Holding on to money possessively, we shall die without ever having used it for a charitable purpose, and our hoarding will have been in vain. If we possess the gem of generosity, however, then even if we have only one dollar, we shall share it with someone else. Without generosity our wealth never really increases, but if we are generous, the more we give away, the more comes back. However, we must strike a balance, because if we give too much away, we may not have enough for our own needs, and this will only lead to unnecessary difficulties. We should follow a middle way, not allowing ourselves to be unduly preoccupied about money.

By having the gem of hearing and studying the Dharma we obtain knowledge about the methods of practice. We do not need a box to hold such an ornament or a horse on which to load it. In fact, even if we were imprisoned but possessed of the gem of hearing, we would be completely relaxed and able to utilize the situation fruitfully in meditation. Accumulation of ordinary wealth, on the other hand, would be of no help in such a situation.

If we have the gem of consideration, we shall always think about how our actions affect others and shall always take them into consideration. Without concern for others, our actions are never justified. This also implies an openness to criticism from others.

To possess the gem of a sense of shame, or personal integrity, will protect us from doing wrong because of our embarrassment at others seeing our selfishness. Normally, we would not act badly in front of others because of this sense of shame, but we may feel free to do so when alone. However, if this sense of shame extends to the Three Supreme Jewels, from whom nothing is hidden, then we shall be certain to restrain ourselves from unskillful deeds at all times. This leads to increased awareness, the avoidance of unwholesome actions, and a feeling of regret at our unskillful deeds of the past.

With the last gem, that of intelligent awareness, we are able to discriminate between beneficial actions and emotional afflictions. Our present actions are determined by the force of our previous ones; to act out of emotional afflictions clouds our pure view of things and is the direct cause of suffering. With intelligence we can exercise awareness in our actions, thereby avoiding those that lead to confusion and misery.

From the spiritual point of view, we are progressing well if we have the awakening mind as our friend and these seven gems as our wealth. Rechungpa once requested his master, Milarepa, for permission to go to Lhasa in central Tibet. At first Milarepa refused, but then finally he gave his consent. After Rechungpa had departed, Milarepa was saddened. When asked why, he said, "My moonlike disciple has gone away, and I, like a dog,

stay behind." When he was further asked what wealth and companions were sent along with his disciple, Milarepa replied,

> I sent him away with the wealth of the seven gems and
> the friend of the awakening mind. I have no worries
> about his safety now.

These seven gems never decrease, for their value remains with
us always. However, we should never speak about them to those
who are unreceptive to spiritual principles. This includes people
who insist that happiness will be found only through material-
ism, and nonhuman beings such as spirits and ghosts, whose
karma prevents them from wisely utilizing such valuable advice.

> *Examine your speech when amid many people.*
> *Examine your mind when living alone.*

45

When with others, we should be mindful not to harm them by
careless remarks. One of the Kadam masters said,

> We make personal judgments and accusations as if they
> were all true. I wish there were locks on my mouth and
> on everyone else's as well.

When alone we should examine our thoughts. Without the
attainment of single-pointed concentration our mind is like
a restless child, but even before we attain single-pointedness,
we should always try to bring our mind back to a state of stable
concentration. The story is often told of a merchant who, during
his meditation, would think about his business so that he could
formulate how to instruct his employees. Whenever he rose
from his meditation, however, he would forget what he had
devised and would soon return to his contemplation. Making
plans during meditation can easily become so habitual that

we achieve a certain false sense of enjoyment from time spent "meditating." We must avoid such gross mental wandering.

The teachings outlined in this text are not solely for Dharma practitioners but can help anyone who simply wishes to lead a good life. Whether or not we accept such doctrines as past and future lives, if we act as if they did exist, there will be only benefit for ourselves and others. We should be friendly toward others yet at the same time as stubborn as an ox when it comes to maintaining the purity of our practices.

There is a Tibetan proverb, "Wrap the rope from your nose around your head." Animals who are lead by a rope through their nose are forced to follow where others lead them. However, if this rope is wrapped around their own head, they remain docile and friendly, free to roam where they wish. In a similar manner, if we wrap the rope of ethical discipline around our own head, it is unnecessary to follow some outer imposition of morality. If our discipline comes from within us, we need no external authorities as guides.

Dharma practice should not be done as mere ritual, out of obligation, or because it is popular. We should not follow Buddhism because it has a growing reputation or has become a "trend," but because we realize its benefits. No matter what practices we do, if they help our mind, they are worthwhile. This in turn helps all others.

This completes the commentary to
The Jewel Rosary of a Bodhisattva.

PART TWO

The Seven-Point Thought Transformation

composed by
the virtuous spiritual friend
of the Kadam tradition
Geshe Chekawa

with commentary
based on an oral transmission by
Geshe Rabten

The Seven-Point Thought Transformation

Om Svasti.

Homage to great compassion.

The essence of this nectar of advice is in continuity
  from Serlingpa.

One

First train in all the preliminary practices.

Two

Having gained stability, receive the secret teaching.

Consider all phenomena as a dream.

Examine the nature of unborn awareness.

The remedy itself is released in its own place.

Place your meditation on the nature of the
  foundation of all: the essence of the path.

In the meditation break be a creator of illusion.

It is like a diamond, the sun, and the healing tree.

When the five degenerations flourish,
  transform them into the path to full awakening.

Banish the one object of every blame.

Meditate on the great kindness of all.

Practice a combination of both giving and taking.

Commence taking progressively from your own side.

Place these two astride the breath.

There are three objects, three poisons, and three
  sources of virtue.

Remember this by repeated recollection.
Practice every activity by these words.

Three
When the container and its contents are filled with
   evil, change this adverse circumstance into the path
   to full awakening.
Utilize every immediate circumstance for meditation.
Possess the four preparations, the highest of means.

Four
Gather together the abridged quintessence of this advice.
Blend the practice of one life with the five forces.
The instruction for the Great Vehicle transmigration
   of consciousness is to apply those very five forces,
   lying in the perfect position.
All Dharma collects into one intention.
Retain the two witnesses of foremost importance.

Five
One is always accompanied by only joyful thoughts.
A reversed attitude indicates a transformation.
One is trained if one is capable, even when distracted.

Six
Always practice the three general points.
Change your attitude while remaining natural.
Speak not of the shortcomings of others.
Think not about whatever is seen in others.
Purify first whichever affliction is heaviest.
Give up all hope of reward.

Abandon poisonous food.

Do not serve the central object leniently.

Be indifferent toward malicious jokes.

Do not lie in ambush.

Never strike at the heart.

Do not load an ox with the load of a dzo.

Do not compete by a last-minute sprint.

Do not be treacherous.

Do not bring a god down to a devil.

Do not inflict misery for possession of happiness.

Seven

Practice all yogas or activities by means of the one yoga.

Practice every suppression of interference by one thought.

There are two duties: at the beginning and the end.

Endure whichever situation arises, either good or bad.

Guard both points more preciously than your life.

Practice the three hardships.

Attain the three principal causes.

Meditate on the three undeclining attitudes.

Possess the three inseparables.

Always practice with pure impartiality on all objects.

Cherish the in-depth and broad application of all skills.

Always meditate on those closely related.

Depend not upon other circumstances.

Exert yourself, especially at this time.

Do not follow inverted deeds.

Do not be erratic.

Do not underestimate your ability.

Be liberated by these two: examination and analysis.

Do not be boastful.

Do not retaliate.

Do not be fickle.

Do not wish for gratitude.

Before practicing I examine my expanding actions;
   then because of many of my wishes,
     having undergone suffering, insults, and criticism,
     I requested the instruction for taming self-
     grasping.

Now if I die, I have no regrets.

THE COMMENTARY TO
The Seven-Point Thought Transformation

Introduction

Om Svasti. Homage to great compassion.

There are many ways of transforming the mind. The method presented here is intended to turn the mind from nonvirtue to virtue. For instance, if we set about training our body, first we feel stiff and awkward. After performing physical exercises, however, our body becomes supple and agile and can adopt many postures that previously would have been difficult. It is evident that the body can gain a greater degree of flexibility by applying the appropriate exercises, and the same is true for the mind. Initially, we may have to endure many difficulties and hardships, but by making a concerted effort we can make our mind very supple. Endowed with this quality we may then engage in a great many skillful activities.

The Tibetan term for thought transformation, *lojong*, literally means "to change our thoughts from one state to another." The method specifically outlined in this text is designed to free our thoughts from self-centered attitudes. Having then acquired a new frame of mind directed to the benefit of all beings, we shall be able to dedicate ourselves totally to their happiness.

The essence of this nectar of advice is in continuity from Serlingpa.

The thought transformation teachings have a sound scriptural basis and derive from Buddha Shakyamuni himself. Their source is found in the various sutras the Buddha preached. These teachings were transmitted through an unbroken succession of accomplished meditation masters of India and were eventually compiled by the great pandit Atisha. Atisha, having studied with over one hundred and fifty spiritual teachers, traveled from northern India to the distant island of Sumatra, where he remained for twelve years near his spiritual master Serlingpa. It was from Serlingpa that he received the lineage of the extensive teachings on developing the awakening mind, or bodhichitta.

Atisha remained in Tibet for the last seventeen years of his life, and he transmitted these teachings on thought transformation to his closest Tibetan disciple, Dromtönpa. They were then handed down through the Kadam geshes Potowa, Langri Tangpa, and Sharawa to Chekawa (A.D. 1102–1176), who compiled them into the easily comprehensible form presented here.

One of the main reasons that prompted Geshe Chekawa to write this text was that he had once read in the *Thought Transformation in Eight Stanzas* a specific verse that said that you should accept all blame and suffering onto yourself and give away all profit, gain, and happiness to others. Intrigued by this unusual idea he traveled to Lhasa, the capital of Tibet, in search of the master who held the oral tradition of the thought transformation teachings and who would be able to explain this verse to him. After arriving in Lhasa and circumambulating the main temple, he inquired who was the master who could teach him the text. When he finally found the town where the author had lived, however, he learned that Langri Tangpa had already passed away.

He then traveled to the monastery of Geshe Sharawa, a renowned teacher who had been a disciple of Langri Tangpa. When he arrived, he found Sharawa giving a discourse on the Hinayana path of the hearers (the *shravaka* vehicle). Confused and disappointed at the lack of any mention of the awaening mind, he felt that he still must search further for a teaching on these two lines. Therefore, when the discourse was over, he waited for Sharawa to pass the retreat house of the monastery as he made his customary afternoon circumambulation. Geshe Chekawa spread a cloth on the ground and called to Geshe Sharawa as he approached, "Please sit. I have some questions to ask you concerning Dharma."

Indignant at being stopped, Geshe Sharawa replied, "I cut all doubts leaving nothing unclear when I gave the discourse before. Where were you then, and what more do you have to ask?"

Chekawa then explained to him about the lines from the book and asked whether it had any substantial reference. He explained that if it had, his only desire was to learn about it. To this Geshe Sharawa answered, "Whether you like to study it or not, if you want to attain complete buddhahood, you must understand its meaning. The scriptural authority of this line is a verse from the *Precious Garland*[7] by the superior Nagarjuna."

After they parted, Chekawa read the text by Nagarjuna and was convinced that the lines in the *Thought Transformation in Eight Stanzas* did indeed have a sound reference. He returned to see Sharawa and asked if he could spend more time with him in the study of its meaning; Sharawa agreed. Then Chekawa asked why Geshe Sharawa had not spoken about the awakening mind when he had given the discourse. In a mood of despair, Sharawa replied that since so few people were genuinely interested in generating the awakening mind, there was no use in explaining what he knew of it to anyone else.

Nevertheless, Chekawa spent almost twelve years with Sharawa and received the full teachings on thought transformation. In addition, he meditated intensively, putting all he had learned into practice. In this way, he developed a deep experience of the awakening mind and became a true awakening warrior, a *bodhisattva*.[8] Out of his infinite compassion for all sentient beings, he condensed all he had learned into his own composition, the *Seven-Point Thought Transformation*.

I

The Preliminary Practices

First train in all the preliminary practices.

The following four subjects for contemplation are the basis of all Dharma instructions: (a) the precious human form, (b) death and impermanence, (c) actions and their results, and (d) the faults of cyclic existence. We should meditate thoroughly on these four points and try to realize them correctly from the very beginning of our practice. If we fail to do this, our meditation will lack a firm foundation, and it will be impossible to realize the more profound aspects, such as the relative and ultimate awakening mind. Just as a person who wishes to become a schoolteacher and teach others effectively must first gain the prerequisites by following the appropriate studies, so must we first engage in all the preliminary practices in order to attain higher realizations.

To ensure the success of any meditation that we practice, we should always prepare by taking sincere refuge in the Three Rare and Supreme Jewels: the fully awakened being (the Buddha), the truth (the Dharma), and those intent on virtue, or the spiritual community (the Sangha). When meditating, try to sit in the full adamantine posture with legs crossed, the feet resting on the opposite thighs or calves, the hands placed in the lap, the spine straight, the eyes slightly opened and focused along the nose, and the mouth relaxed with the tongue pressed gently against the palate.[9]

Prior to the main meditation, we shall discover many extraneous thoughts breaking like a storm into our mind. Since these must be eliminated for any successful contemplation, we should initially practice simple breath awareness. First, as we breathe out, visualize very fine smoke coming up from the heart and out through the nostrils. Then as we inhale, visualize this fine smoke reentering gradually and evenly. While placing the concentration on the breath in this way, there are four things to avoid: breathing so heavily that we can hear our breath going in and out, giving effort to breathing, breathing out so far that we have to suck back in quickly, and breathing too rapidly. In doing this initial meditation, our mindfulness should ride on the wind of the breath like a person rides a horse. It should not be distracted to one side or the other.

60

Placing the mind on the breath is like looking down on a busy marketplace and watching the movements of just one person. The confused bustle gradually fades into the background. It is up to the individual to determine when these extraneous thoughts have been pacified and to realize whether or not firmness of concentration has been achieved. For some people it takes only seven or twenty-one rounds of breathing to reduce internal gossip, but for others it may take much longer. When a state of mental stability has been attained, we can proceed to the more advanced objects of contemplation, because now the mind will be more able to remain on them steadily.

The Precious Human Form

We should realize that there is nothing that we cannot accomplish if we put to good use our precious human life. We have this potential because human beings are endowed with a special intelligence not possessed by other beings, and it is through the power of this intelligence that anything becomes possible. Yet, though all human beings are born with this intelligence, many do not use it well, and some even misuse it, continually wasting their potential on unnecessary worldly diversions. If the human life is used for a mundane purpose, no matter how far-reaching it may be, that purpose always has a limit. However, by harnessing this intelligence to spiritual development, it can lead to complete freedom from confusion—the fully awakened state, which is separated from all obstacles and pain and is endowed with infinite virtuous qualities.

Initially, it is most important to realize that all people have this ability, or potential, and power of mind within them. If a precious treasure is buried on your land, you must first realize it is there before you can use it. In the same way we must realize that we have the precious treasure of discriminating intelligence within us; only then can we take full advantage of it. Just as a person who discovers buried treasure can use it for material benefit, we can use our precious human form to benefit ourselves infinitely in a spiritual way.

All beings desire happiness and want to avoid suffering, but to use this life for mere material gratification leads to only greater dissatisfaction. To eliminate suffering, we should not delay in applying our life to following the principles of an inner path. In order to follow this path now and achieve the happiness we desire, it is important to realize how extremely fortunate we are in having gained the eighteen unique qualities of a precious human birth. These eighteen comprise the eight freedoms from birth in detrimental realms or situations where there is no leisure for any spiritual practice,[10] and the ten endowments of beneficial circumstances.[11] If we fail to take the Dharma to heart after having attained this complete set of opportunities, it will be very difficult to gain this chance again. Moreover, this providential occasion can be suddenly lost in death.

DEATH AND IMPERMANENCE

The impermanence of life is no secret; it is clearly evident to everyone. Now that we have attained a human form endowed with basic intelligence, we should not postpone using it for the practice of inner development. Our life will not last forever. Moreover, we can never be certain when the end of this precious opportunity will come. It makes no difference what our rank, age, or state of health may be; the circumstances of death are many. Therefore, it is sheer foolishness to postpone Dharma practice by thinking that for the time being we are too busy, or that later, when we have more free time, we shall start. Since we do have good health, strength, and all the necessary facilities, we should take advantage of this opportunity without delay.

Our physical environment can be a powerful teacher; if we are constantly aware of our surroundings, we shall observe impermanence in everything. Human beings have no special qualities that exempt them from being subject to impermanence. In fact, we are all like sheep in a slaughterhouse; it makes no difference which goes first because eventually all will die. Although most of us are quite certain that death will come, since we have no idea when this event will occur we must train ourselves to develop mindfulness of the uncertainty of the time of our death. This awareness is one of our best teachers because it reminds us not to be lazy or to waste our time and is a constant force adding momentum to our practice.

ACTIONS AND THEIR RESULT

The reason we practice Dharma is to attain the fully purified state of buddhahood, and if we do not achieve this state during our present lifetime, we should continue to pursue this aim throughout all future lifetimes until it is reached. If we practice as much as possible in this life, we shall acquire a certain power or positive energy that will carry over to the next life. If we then spend the next life in practice, the force of both lives will combine to affect the life after that. This cumulative process is like the life of a fruit tree—in its first year of growth it is small and yields nothing; only after several years of careful attention does it mature and bear fruit.

Therefore, to be able to benefit others we must realize that to be born as a human being endowed with the eighteen unique conditions is a very precious opportunity. With a human birth, we have a chance to practice Dharma, which we could not do if we were born an animal. Moreover, such a favorable birth is not a mere coincidence but the result of specific causes—the abandoning of unskillful actions and the accumulation of skillful ones.

We receive only the fruit of those actions that we ourselves have created. If we act carelessly, following the impulses of emotional afflictions such as greed, aggression, arrogance, and so forth, we shall only produce results opposite to our wishes. The results of careless actions will eliminate any chance we may have of finding circumstances conducive to spiritual practice in the future.

Understanding our actions (our *karma*) is a profound and vast subject containing many aspects. In general, actions are produced through the three doors of our body, speech, and mind. In order to avoid suffering and confusion in the future and to acquire a precious human form again, we must cease creating any more unwholesome actions; specifically we should stop what are called the "ten nonvirtuous actions." Instead, we should constantly act with skillful awareness, for this will help in the achievement of the happiness we desire.

To take advantage of the freedoms and endowments of a precious human form, we should adopt as the foundation of our life the abandonment of the ten nonvirtuous actions. Abandoning the ten nonvirtuous actions naturally corresponds with the practice of the ten virtuous ones. There are three unskillful actions of the body: killing any sentient being, taking that which is not given, and engaging in sexual misconduct. There are four of speech: lying, slandering or creating division between people, speaking harshly by scolding, swearing, or being sarcastic, and foolishly chattering or engaging in senseless conversation. There are three unwholesome actions of the mind: greed, hatred, or ill-will toward others, and holding on to such wrong views as disbelief in the law of cause and effect or in the attainment of the fully awakened state of buddhahood.

When we understand that committing these ten unwholesome deeds causes the most harm and the deepest suffering to ourselves as well as to others, we come to think of them as our most dangerous enemy. If any impulse arises to commit even one of them, we should quickly analyze the deceptive nature and detrimental results of such an impulse. In this way we shall be able to prevent ourselves from committing the action, and eventually stop the impulse from arising. The successful abandonment of these becomes the practice of the ten virtuous deeds, and this in itself accumulates much positive merit.

We should regard the desire to commit any of the ten unwholesome deeds as more harmful than a poisonous snake coiled in our lap. If a snake were to bite us, the worst it could do would be to cause pain, illness, and possibly death; it does not have the power to propel our consciousness at death into an unfavorable birth. Committing any of the nonvirtuous deeds, however insignificant it might appear, does have such power. Therefore, accumulating instincts for committing any unskillful actions has consequences more dire than any bite by a venomous snake.

THE FAULTS OF CYCLIC EXISTENCE

The whole of cyclic existence (*samsara*) is like a prison, but if we do not understand its unsatisfactoriness, we shall never try to gain release from it and attain ultimate liberation.

There are six general types of suffering that pervade all realms within this cycle. The first is the suffering of the uncertainty of friends, wealth, and social position within the span of one lifetime. A person who was once an employer may easily become an employee, or nations that were once at war may become allies. Second is the misery of never being satisfied: we may have what is necessary, but we always crave more; having achieved one goal, we strive after still another. We are never content with what we have. If we are always dissatisfied, even though we may be materially wealthy we shall live in a state of mental poverty.

Third is the suffering of indefinite rebirths. We have already passed through countless lives and abandoned so many previous bodies that were we to collect them together they would make a mountain. The next, the repeated suffering of conception, means that again and again we shall have to be conceived and take a form; this very process is always in the nature of suffering. Unless we free ourselves, we shall cycle endlessly.

Next is the misery of fluctuation: after accumulation comes depletion, after being high comes the fall, after meeting comes parting, after life comes death. The final suffering is that of being alone at birth, in illness, and at death. When we enter and leave this life, we do so alone; the only things that accompany us are the propensities from the skillful or unskillful deeds we have committed in this and previous lifetimes.

In addition to these six general types, there are three great sufferings. The first, the suffering of suffering, is clearly understood by all beings to be misery: it arises from physical suffering and includes pain, sickness, sadness, birth, aging, and death. However, the second, the suffering of change caused by the transitory nature of all things, is not generally regarded as suffering since it is commonly mistaken for true happiness. For instance, most people consider that the mundane goals that produce security in the form of material comfort and goods are sufficient for happiness and peace of mind. Without realizing the suffering caused by change, people cling to these objects as permanent entities capable of producing lasting contentment. However, the instability inherent in all things soon causes such people distress when they again have to change to something "new" in order to keep up with current standards or find new sources of comfort. It is like alleviating the discomfort of heat by moving to a cold place that, after some time, itself becomes uncomfortable. This type of suffering encompasses anything that appears to give pleasure yet changes into dissatisfaction.

The third is called all-pervasive suffering because compositional relationships (*samskara*) pervade all of cyclic existence. Although this is a far more subtle and more difficult concept to comprehend than the previous two, it is the foundation upon which all suffering lies. Unless we recognize this all-pervasive suffering, escape from cyclic existence is impossible. However, by deeply contemplating this suffering, the other two great sufferings, and the six general sufferings, we shall become completely disgusted with the round of birth, death, and rebirth, and a strong renunciation of and detachment from the entire cycle of existence will develop, together with the wish to find a way out.

Therefore, it is essential for any spiritual practitioner to recognize suffering, the first Noble Truth that Buddha Shakyamuni taught. Although Buddha has also shown the path by which we may attain cessation of this suffering, if we do not first face up to this reality of our existence, we shall never desire to free ourselves from it.

The *preliminary practices* refer to meditation on these four topics, which turns the mind away from worldliness, and other activities, such as making prostrations and mandala offerings, reciting the purification mantra of Vajrasattva together with the corresponding meditation, and guru yoga, the practice of union with one's spiritual master.[12]

We should do more than just study these teachings and understand them intellectually; we should meditate on them and apply the resultant insights to daily activities. First, we should look around us and try to understand in terms of the teachings what is happening in our environment. We should then utilize this awareness in our meditation in order to develop an intuitive realization and deep conviction that these teachings are in fact true. We should not merely expend all our energy collecting pieces of information, but make an effort to experience their validity through insight in our daily life. If we do not practice in this way, we shall be like a person who goes into every shop, asks the price of goods and compares their quality, but having no money is never able to buy anything. If we listen to spiritual teachings carefully, learn them well, and then put them into practice in order to gain realization of their validity, our work is worthwhile and will definitely be fruitful.

2

The Main Practice

At the center of the transformational psychology of training the mind is the practice of activating the awakening mind—bodhichitta—which, like all phenomena, has two aspects: ultimate and conventional. The first aspect involves developing the right view, or the realization of emptiness *(shunyata)*. The second, the conventional awakening mind, itself has two aspects: cultivating the altruistic aspiration to attain the fully awakened state of mind, and then venturing into the actual practices and meditations in order to attain it. In many other Mahayana texts the conventional awakening mind is explained first, but here the method is reversed. Both orders are correct, and our practice can follow either.

1. GENERATING THE ULTIMATE AWAKENING MIND

Having gained stability, receive the secret teaching.

Prior to receiving the secret teaching on the ultimate awakening mind, it is essential to be well-prepared and have full conviction in and complete understanding of the fundamental topics, such as actions and their consequences, the suffering of cyclic existence, and impermanence. After having gained firmness and stability in these, we can safely be instructed in the secret teaching; without this firm basis, there will be the danger of falling into the extreme of nihilism.

Of all the teachings of Buddha Shakyamuni, emptiness is the most difficult to understand. Each of the four main philosophical schools of Buddhism (the *Vaibhashika, Sautrantika, Chittamatra,* and *Madhyamaka*) has a different level of understanding of emptiness according to the degree of precision with which they comprehend it. The most subtle view is expressed by the Middle Way (*Madhyamaka*) school of philosophy founded by Nagarjuna. Since the comprehension of emptiness is difficult and, if misunderstood, even treacherous, Nagarjuna has said in his *Fundamental Treatise Called Wisdom,*

> Viewing emptiness mistakenly,
> like grabbing a snake incorrectly,
> brings ruin to those of little intelligence.[13]

A. THE MEDITATION PERIOD

(i) Discerning the object of refutation

Within the cycle of existence myriad beings are oppressed with suffering because they continually carry within themselves the root of countless emotional afflictions. The single root of all mental afflictions is the ignorance that grasps at phenomena as being inherently or independently existent. This is known as the self-grasping ignorance (*atmagraha-avidya*). Therefore, meditation on emptiness is explained here first because it is the most powerful opponent for eliminating this self-grasping ignorance. In a battle, soldiers try to kill each other, but they especially aim to kill the opposing leader. In the same way, the main aim of Dharma practice should be to destroy the self-grasping ignorance within oneself because this is the root of all suffering.

Basically it is said that there are two kinds of self-grasping ignorance: holding the idea of a self or substantial ego-identity in relation to our own being, and holding the idea of an inherent identity in relation to other phenomena.

Meditation on emptiness is not just making the mind completely blank and empty of all thoughts. Rather, an effort must be made in the beginning stages of meditation to discover the nature of the ignorance that is grasping the concept of a self and understand exactly how it functions. Only then can we discover the falsity, or emptiness, of this ignorance. In the same way that shooting an arrow without clearly seeing the target accomplishes nothing, meditating on emptiness without recognizing the concept of a self-identity is meaningless. The following is a brief explanation of the way in which everything appears because of ignorance.

It may be that some of us already have some intellectual understanding that at present our minds view phenomenal appearances in a mistaken manner. We may even make such statements as, "Oh, what I perceive does not exist in the way I now see it, but really exists in some other way." Yet most of us have no true appreciation of the full implication of such words, and we continue to believe that we ourselves, and all external phenomena as well, exist as independent units or things. If someone were to ask us if anything could possibly exist independently all by itself, we would be forced to answer that despite conventional appearances, nothing actually exists in this way. Nevertheless, most of us still feel deeply that whatever we perceive appears to exist independently by itself.

For instance, when reading the words on this page, we automatically tend to think that they exist independently from their own side. We do not take into consideration their relationship to ourselves, the factor of our consciousness, or our manner of perceiving them. Holding on to the concept of independent existence, we continue to read without awareness of the interdependence of things. This applies to all phenomena we perceive. However, this appearance of all external objects and of our own person as being independent entities is merely superficial and does not withstand analysis. If we search thoroughly for the underlying mode of existence—the actual nature of reality—then the appearance of things as independent entities gradually loses its clarity until finally it disappears.

Generally this false idea that external phenomena exist independently is no different from the way most of us view ourselves, thinking that we too exist independently. Usually it is unclear to us how the belief in an ego-identity within our person actually operates, but when strong emotions such as joy, sorrow, hatred, and fear arise, it is easier to perceive.

For instance, if the police were to arrest us unjustly, we would experience an intense emotional reaction. On such an occasion, we would find a very strong "I" expressed by a thought such as "I cannot be arrested like this!" When this happens, we must forget our accusers and instead look within ourselves to examine this "I" that seems to exist by itself, independent of body and mind. Such a situation presents an excellent opportunity to find and analyze our concept of a self.

By regularly observing the way our ego functions and also by analyzing the way we grasp at outer objects as having some sort of self-existence, we shall eventually realize that while all phenomena seem to have a true existence, this appearance is merely the product of our ignorance—in nature, like a dream. Therefore the text reads:

Consider all phenomena as a dream.

Dreams sometimes appear to be totally realistic, especially nightmares in which, for example, a fierce animal attacks us or some frightening apparition pursues us. When dreaming, everything seems to have physical reality and to be fully capable of causing benefit, suffering, or fear. In fact, a nightmare may be so vivid that we suddenly awaken, panting and drenched in perspiration. However, all that we feel and see in a dream is merely illusory and does not have any real or true existence.

In the same way, when we feel strong emotions arise, we are presented with a special opportunity to look within and clearly observe how the appearance of the ego-identity relating to our person is grasped by our ignorance. This ignorance itself is like a dream—an illusion deeply rooted within ourselves. It usually holds on to the idea of a self in relation to everything, but under special, emotionally charged circumstances it grasps at an independent identity more intensely than usual and can thus be observed more clearly. Under calmer conditions we cannot see how it operates because it is very subtle.

The initial step in the meditation on emptiness is to spend many months simply trying to recognize the object of ignorance and see how ignorance functions by grasping on to the self. Only after we have gained this understanding shall we be able to refute this object and not be swayed by the detrimental influence of grasping at it. Seeing the emptiness of the object of ignorance, then, is a way to approach an understanding of the true meaning of emptiness. To meditate without this initial understanding, not recognizing the object that is to be refuted, and to think that emptiness is like the empty space in a room, will never lead to complete realization, since this is not at all the meaning of ultimate truth.

If a thief mingled with a group of people in a house, first we would have to track him down before we could expel him and confidently assert that the house was empty of thieves.

Similarly, in order to understand emptiness, which is the direct refutation of the self-grasping ignorance, first we must recognize the object of this ignorance and the manner in which such ignorance holds on to both our own personality and all outer phenomena as being self-existent. Merely to read, listen to, or study teachings on emptiness without regularly meditating on it will never lead to direct and intuitive realization.

The first point of this meditation is to see how ignorance grasps at an ego-identity of our own being. Only after familiarizing ourselves with this can we turn our meditation toward examining the concept of how all outer phenomena seem to exist in the same way—that is, as independently existing selves or units. Thus, we should examine how we perceive all things through the five sensory bases (eye, ear, nose, tongue, and body) in relation to the five sensory objects (forms, sounds, smells, tastes, and objects of touch). With increased awareness of how our ego and ignorance function, we shall come to see the fallacy of our present mode of perception.

The way in which all external objects appear to exist independently, by themselves, without any relationship to our perception or the mental labels we impute on them, is the view of ignorance. In truth, there is nothing whatsoever that exists in this way. We are convinced everything has true, inherent, independent self-existence because our mind is obscured by ignorance. Desire, greed, hatred, pride, and all other afflictions of the mind arise from this mistaken view.

Even though the images that appear in dreams seem to be very real, they are actually illusions of our mind. Likewise, viewing each phenomenon as existing by itself, completely independent of its surroundings, causes, conditions, and our mental labeling of it, is the same as regarding dreams as real. This view, although apparently based on reality, is completely mistaken and unfounded. However, the analogy of dreams should not be applied too thoroughly: the images that appear in dreams have no objective existence at all, and if we apply this same reasoning directly to our nonsleeping state, thinking that although animals and other objects do appear to our senses, they in fact do not exist at all, we then fall into the nihilist extreme. Such a false conclusion as the belief in complete nonexistence is a dangerous and perverted view; holding it is like grasping a venomous snake by the tail.

The comparison of reality to a dream, therefore, is based on this point: that contrary to our ignorant conception, neither ourselves nor other objects have any independent self-existence, just as images in a dream have none. This negation of independent, or inherent, existence is not the negation of existence itself. If we did not exist, we could neither meditate nor realize the view of emptiness, nor could we come into contact with various objects and situations. If we do not exist, then who is it who thinks we do not exist? We do exist, but not in the manner our ignorance leads us to believe.

If, for example, we were to look at a snowy mountain while wearing yellow sunglasses, it would appear yellow, but when we took them off, this illusion would disappear, and we would see the snow as white. Similarly, all phenomena appear to exist independent of their causes, conditions, and the mode of our perception of them because our perception and consciousness are obscured by the affliction of the self-grasping ignorance. This covering of ignorance is like the yellow sunglasses that obscure our vision, for just as the snow does exist, but not with a yellow color, all phenomena seen as truly self-existent still do exist, but not independently.

Trying to realize emptiness is like walking across a narrow and treacherous track with deep snow on either side. In order to negotiate the way safely we have to be alert and skillful so as not to fall to either side. In meditating on emptiness we should skillfully avoid falling into either of the two extreme views. The first is the affirming extreme, which is a firm adherence to the view of self-grasping ignorance. This belief in the self-identity, of both phenomena and our person, will lead to the amplification of the ego. The other wrong view is the nihilist extreme: through reasoning that the view of ignorance is mistaken, we reach a conclusion that everything is nonexistent. Therefore, we must protect ourselves from both faults and exercise skill in following the middle way. We must maintain full concentration on the emptiness of self-existence and not on mere nothingness. To meditate on the outright negation of existence is completely wrong.

We have been caught in the cycle of confusion since beginningless time and have become so completely accustomed to it that we now feel inseparable from the ignorance that holds us here. We cannot differentiate between the deluded conceptions of ignorance and the true mode of existence. Instead, we believe that our perception, which is in fact based on a lack of awareness, is the only way of relating to the appearances of the phenomenal world. Yet, just as images in a dream have no substantial existence, our emotional afflictions—which arise from the ignorant concept that all phenomena exist independent of their causes, parts, and our imputation of them—also do not exist in truth. When we speak of the emptiness of phenomena, what is it they are empty of? They are empty of independent self-existence.

(ii) The emptiness of the mind

Examine the nature of unborn awareness.

Although it is difficult to realize emptiness, it is possible, by meditating on our own being and on outer phenomena, to recognize the invalidity of our ignorant concept of self-existence. However, a further complication remains, because our conception of independent existence also applies very powerfully to the mind that is meditating. When such a difficulty arises, we must concentrate on consciousness itself in order to perceive that the mind, too, is empty and does not exist independently.

The mind has not come from somewhere, like a guest who has come into a room, nor does it go anywhere. It has no form or color and does not abide in any definite place. In fact, it is completely intangible and depends on only two things—the object that is perceived and the senses through which that object is perceived.

Through constant observation of the mind in this way we shall see that it does not exist in the way we previously conceived it to. When we had thought that our mind was meditating, it always seemed as though we could hold on to and isolate this concept, but after meditating as described we shall recognize the emptiness of this previous ignorant conception. However, this emptiness does not imply that mind does not exist, but rather that there is no mind that can be grasped and isolated. Since it does exist, we are able to use it for meditation.

(iii) The emptiness of emptiness

The remedy itself is released in its own place.

After meditating for some time on outer phenomena and also on the consciousness that is meditating, we should attain an insight into emptiness. However, with this limited insight, another wrong concept leading to difficulties will arise, because emptiness itself will then appear to be independently existent. At such a time, we should meditate on emptiness itself in the same way.

Emptiness does not exist by itself, because it is completely dependent on its base. Without this base of emptiness, there can be no emptiness. For example, this page or any other phenomenon is known as the base of emptiness. Since the base, or this page, is not independently self-existent, its essential nature is empty. However, emptiness also does not exist independently by itself because it too is dependent on the base and cannot possibly exist by itself. As it is said in the *Heart of Wisdom Discourse*:

> O Shariputra, form here is emptiness and emptiness
> indeed is form. Emptiness is not different from form;
> form is not different from emptiness. What is form,
> that is emptiness; what is emptiness, that is form.
> The same applies to feeling, recognition, karmic
> formations, and consciousness.

One example traditionally used for nonexistence is the horn of a rabbit. Since this base—in this case the horn of a rabbit—is completely nonexistent, we can never speak of its emptiness. Both emptiness and the base of emptiness, form and so forth, totally depend on each other in a way similar to two planks of wood leaning together and giving mutual support to each other. Without one, the other will fall down.

The realization of emptiness is the most effective remedy for curing the chronic disease of ignorance. However, holding the remedy to be something exceptional and self-existent is one of the grossest ignorant conceptions. The remedy itself must also dissolve into emptiness and be released in itself.

When we begin to approach meditation on emptiness, we

should apply the meditation to our own ego-identity, then later transfer that awareness to the concept of self-existence in relation to outer phenomena, including the mind that is meditating. Finally, we should direct our insight toward emptiness itself. After meditating on these aspects progressively, we should meditate on them collectively, trying to keep the mind stabilized on the negation of our ignorant conceptions for as long as possible. Six examples are traditionally given to assist the meditator in maintaining concentration on emptiness.

1. Like the sunlight that brightly illuminates all the land, the mind should not be dark and dull but bright, clear, and alert; the mind should be illuminated and radiant.

2. Like the stillness of the deep and vast ocean which, unlike a small stream or river, is not easily agitated, the mind should be kept calm and tranquil, far away from any agitation.

3. Just as a young child's reaction on first viewing intricate temple murals is without any discrimination as to good or bad, all our concentration should be unwaveringly maintained on emptiness without discriminating about its depth or profundity. Just as the child stares wide-eyed at the painting, we should view emptiness with the eye of intelligent awareness fully open.

4. In the same way that eagles can soar high in the sky with little exertion, while needing to flap their wings only occasionally, we should stay aloft in the space of emptiness, only once in a while needing to apply intense examination to the nature of the self, when our concentration slips into

boredom or mental dullness. Having applied analytical meditation, we gather the energy to resume meditation placed effortlessly on emptiness. If, like small birds that continually flap their wings yet never rise to great heights, we engage only in this analysis, our overall meditation will never develop. On the other hand, if we make no use of this faculty but remain immersed in emptiness, gradually the power of this meditation will exhaust itself and sleep will overcome us—just as an eagle that never flaps its wings will eventually fall to earth.

5. With regard to extraneous thoughts that arise during meditation, we should relate to them as does a pigeon to a ship that is in the middle of the ocean. If it flies from the ship it may first stray some distance, but since there is only the ocean to be found, it will soon return. In the same way, since trying to suppress stray thoughts that arise during meditation may lead to unnecessary complications, we should allow them to arise and simply observe their nature and development, without getting involved in them. Thus, gradually extraneous thoughts will diminish and the mind will return to the ship, the object of meditation.

6. However, this technique may not always be sufficient, so we should be vigilant for any distracting thoughts, especially emotional afflictions such as fantasies involving desire, aggression, and so forth, and be like a skillful swordsman defending himself from the attack of an archer. In this example, the archer constantly shoots arrows, which the swordsman skillfully deflects with his sword. At such times, the swordsman must concentrate intensely because, if his attention lessens for an instant, he will be struck. Just so,

we should wield the sword of intelligent awareness with complete mindfulness and skill in order to avoid being wounded by the sharp arrows of the emotional afflictions.

Although these six methods may be helpful in meditating, if we do not have a correct idea of what emptiness is, time spent in meditation on it will be completely wasted.

(iv) The spacelike meditation

Place your meditation on the nature of the foundation of all: the essence of the path.

The term "foundation of all" here is a synonym for emptiness. This instruction is the culmination of prior explanations because, after realizing the emptiness of our ignorant conception that things exist independently, we should maintain all energy and attention on this emptiness—the essence of the path and the very foundation of all. We must not expend our energy on sense objects, dissipating it through the five sensory organs.

By sustaining our mind in emptiness, our understanding will gradually become clearer until, after repeated meditation, we shall attain a nonconceptual, or intuitive, realization. The more powerful the realization of emptiness, the weaker the force of ignorance becomes until it finally ends. The clearer our view of the true way in which things exist, the clearer we see the faults and false nature of ignorance. Finally, we shall kick ignorance away; simultaneously, the production of mundane actions and the corresponding creation of instinctive propensities will weaken until they also cease completely.

Keeping our mind placed on the direct negation of the independent self-existence of both the ego and the self-identity of outer phenomena is known as spacelike meditative equipoise. The stronger this is, the purer will be our view while we engage in the activities of the post-meditation period.

B. THE POST-MEDITATION PERIOD

In the meditation break be a creator of illusion.

When we are not formally meditating on emptiness but are engaged in the activities of daily life, such as reading, eating, walking, and working, we should reflect on our mistaken view of all phenomena in the same way that a conjurer regards his own illusory creations. For instance, a conjurer, being a master of illusion, is able to transform one thing into another magically, such as a rock into a bird. Both he and his audience see the bird, but there is an important difference between his attitude and theirs; he is not deceived by his own creation because he knows that it has appeared only as a result of his craft.

In the same way, when we are out of formal meditation on emptiness and again have to experience our external environment, we should regard the mistaken view we have of it, which will still continue to arise, as merely the illusory creation of the ignorant propensities in our mind. Since we have seen previously in the meditational period that the object of such a mistaken view is empty of independent existence, we should regard this deceptive view of things as completely false, just as the conjurer regards his illusory creations.

Most serious emotional afflictions arise not when we are meditating intensively but when we are engaged in daily activities. Therefore, if we treat the appearances of phenomena and our ego with the same attitude as that which a magician has toward his own illusory creations, then even if emotional afflictions

82

do arise, we shall not grasp them with as much ignorance as we would have before we practiced meditation. Such intelligent awareness is extremely precious and will help to diminish the force of the ignorance that clings to the independent existence of all phenomena. Thus, meditation and post-meditation sessions will be mutually beneficial.

C. THE TRUE MODE OF EXISTENCE

If phenomena do not exist in the manner in which we now perceive them, what is their actual mode of existence? Let us each take ourselves as an example and examine our past activities. Who is the person, the "I" who was born, who has grown, traveled, and studied? Who is here? Whose name is this? Who am "I"?

Then we should meditate more objectively by searching deeply. What is the "I," and where is the "I"? We should look for it within this body and this existence. Meditating deeply, we should examine all parts of our body from the top of our head down to the tips of our toes, through our veins, bones, nerves, flesh, and skin, and even between the layers of our skin.

Once we have acquired the certainty that the "I" does not reside in any of these parts of the body, another question will arise. Is the "I" the mind, the consciousness? However, even the mind is not our self. If we look closely at what would follow if this were the case, we discover many contradictions.

For instance, all aspects of the mind can be included in three categories: virtuous, nonvirtuous, and neutral. Now, if the virtuous mind were to be identified as the self, then when it arose, the self would be very strong, and when it diminished, the self would be weak. It would follow that those who are nonvirtuous would have little ego, since such an ego is exclusively the virtuous

83

mind. In the same way, if the self were the nonvirtuous mind, then since this also arises and perishes, it would follow that when a nonvirtuous mind had been eliminated, the ego would also be eliminated.

Furthermore, the unwholesome mind itself can be classified into many additional aspects such as lust, aggression, and so on. Which of these is the self? And if the ego-identity, or self, existed only in the indifferent mind, then whenever a virtuous or nonvirtuous thought arose, the indifferent mind, together with the ego, would disappear. Although there are more subtle means of investigating this "I" in the consciousness, searching in this manner will reveal that the self, or ego, does not exist, not even as the mind, and it is impossible for a self-identity to exist in any third place apart from the body and the mind.

By these means, we shall conclude that although our existence is obvious, the very strong and independent sense of "I" has merely been fabricated by our ignorance and does not actually exist. At that point we may almost decide that perhaps we do not exist at all. However, although the "I" is not findable, we should not be carried away by thoughts of nonexistence. The very fact of our existence allows us to investigate in this way and doubt our existence. Yet exactly how do we exist?

Neither the mind alone nor the body alone is our self. The self arises through the interdependence of body and mind and that aspect of consciousness that identifies such feelings as "I am sick," "I am hungry," and so forth. The conventional appearance of a self comes into existence based upon a special combination of these parts—that is, the body, the mind, and the consciousness that incorporates it all.

Take a watch, for example. None of its parts alone is the watch. None of the cogs, wheels, or springs inside are the watch.

Neither the dial nor either of the two hands is itself a watch. However, when these parts, none of them individually a watch, are gathered together and combined in a certain way, we can apply a mental label and conventionally designate this object a "watch." Similarly, neither the body alone nor the mind alone is our self. But when our consciousness, form, and name combine in a particular relationship with each other, we say that they exist relatively as "I" or "myself."

This has been merely a brief explanation about emptiness, or the negation of the ignorance that grasps at an independent self-identity, together with some meditational methods and techniques. We should approach qualified spiritual teachers who are well versed in this subtle subject and study it more deeply in order to comprehend it, for it requires both much learning and much meditative practice before it can be realized directly. We may now have a slight intellectual understanding of it, but only after having attained an intuitive insight into emptiness shall we become aware of the true mode of existence of all phenomena. Then we shall be able to perceive the conventional and ultimate ways in which things exist. However, the reasoning that leads us to the complete denial of existence is faulty and totally unfounded.

2. ACTIVATING THE CONVENTIONAL AWAKENING MIND

The conventional awakening mind—the aspiration to attain the fully awakened state of buddhahood in order to effectively help free all sentient beings from suffering—is the principal subject of thought transformation. Here it is compared to three objects.

It is like a diamond, the sun, and the healing tree.

Even a small fragment of a diamond surpasses all other jewels because it is the hardest and brightest of them all. Similarly, even when the awakening mind is first developing, it already outshines all the qualities of those self-motivated spiritual practitioners, the arhats—both the hearers and the solitary realizers.[14] Also, just as a fraction of light from the sun has the power to dispel the darkness over the whole land, when the awakening mind starts to rise, so too does it immediately dispel the internal darkness of misery and emotional afflictions. And like the healing tree, which has the power to cure any illness, as soon as the awakening mind arises, it begins to cure the chronic illnesses grounded in those emotional afflictions.

The power of the awakening mind is unique, and activating it during this era of degeneration is especially effective and necessary.

When the five degenerations flourish,
transform them into the path to full awakening.

In this present age, the five degenerations are said to be rife. The first is the *degeneration of the time*. There is little lasting peace on the planet, many nations suffer from internal strife or are at war with each other, and famine and disease prevail throughout many lands. The second is the *degeneration of beings*. The majority of people living in this age hold ideas that are morally wrong, and many people are intolerant of others to the point of hatred. Third is the *degeneration of emotional afflictions*; in this age they have become overwhelmingly gross, for the minds of many people are obsessed with both greed and violence. The fourth is *degeneration of the lifespan*; in this age, increasing dangers to life from accidents and unforeseen calamities have made the age at which death occurs unpredictable. Finally, there is a great *degeneration in the ideologies of people.* Nowadays, wrong views and philosophies are flourishing, especially those encouraging such false beliefs as the denial of cause and effect and the impossibility of buddhahood, the full realization of one's potential.

Although the beings who are alive at this time suffer continuously from confusion and lack of logical and meaningful orientation, the activation of the awakening mind can channel these inauspicious circumstances—as well as any fortunate ones—into a method that will lead to liberation. Therefore, it is both necessary and beneficial to generate the awakening mind and gain an inner weapon with which to defend ourselves from the dangers of this age.

Of the two ways of developing an experience of the awakening mind, the method presented in this text is considered to have special qualities and to be very effective. It is discussed in great detail in *A Guide to the Bodhisattva's Way of Life*[15] by Shantideva, but what follows here will be a concise explanation. When reading such instructions, we should try to assimilate them immediately into our stream of consciousness so that they become one with our mind. Do not regard them as merely a story or a philosophical discourse.

*B*anish the one object of every blame.

Whenever any difficulty or trouble arises, we usually blame it on some other person, some other object. Nations accuse other nations of causing conflict, and even dogs get upset at other dogs. However, it is entirely incorrect to blame someone else because the true enemy deserving this blame is the self-cherishing attitude, which we have always had within us.

We consider ourselves to be very precious and important, and such attachment and dedication lead each of us to commit many unskillful deeds aimed solely at bringing us temporal pleasure and comfort. When we do not possess something we desire or when danger threatens something to which we are attached, we react with aggression and selfishness. By acting in such a self-centered way, we accumulate negative karmic propensities that will arise later as misery.

Even among nations, many unwholesome deeds are perpetrated for similar self-motivated reasons. For instance, a nation with imperialistic attitudes wages war over territories belonging to other people with the motivation of exploiting their resources for its own selfish ends. Conversely, a country will fight to defend itself from external aggression because it fears the loss of its own territory. However, in so doing it creates only more conflict and misery. Even when two small insects fight, their reasons are the same, and we too commit many self-centered actions for similar aggressive or defensive reasons.

In our present situation as human beings born into an era of degeneration, most of us have accumulated strong adverse imprints on our streams of consciousness and thus have many karmic debts to pay. We must recognize that all our faults and problems are actually within us. The principal cause of them is the ignorant self-cherishing attitude that narrows our attention to only one person: our own self. When we feel uncomfortable from even a slight thirst or discomfort in the heat, our self-centered attitude desiring immediate relief from this annoyance leads us to crave a cold drink. Yet our self-cherishing attitude—the true enemy—allows us time for only brief and comparatively unsympathetic thoughts for the numberless beings who have greater misfortunes than we.

The accumulation of karmic debts that we owe other beings can be terminated either through intensive meditation or by our own acceptance of the fruit of such debts. This last method is the easiest and is the technique taught in this text.

We should view any person who appears to be harming us as an intermediary who, in causing us difficulty, frees us from a more serious ripening of our past unskillful actions. In such situations those who harm us are, in reality, our benefactors. We should constantly remember their kindness in showing us, as our spiritual teacher does, that the burdens heaped on us are actually the results of our own actions. For instance, if we had a debt and our creditor told us that to cancel it we need take only a slap in the face, we would see this person as kind for letting us off lightly. In the same way, harm inflicted by others helps us eliminate karmic debts that may otherwise ripen in more serious ways.

Therefore, the true object that we must recognize as our greatest enemy, deserving all the blame for any misery we may experience, is the self-cherishing attitude we hold within us. In addition, we should always remember the kindness of other beings, whatever their character may be. Whether they appear to be harming or aiding us, they are always assisting us in the elimination of accumulated karmic debts. Never think that this is merely a pleasing or euphemistic way of interpreting events, for this is the actual way things are.

*M*editate on the great kindness of all.

If we train our minds to recognize the great kindness of all sentient beings, then despite any physical discomforts we shall always be joyful and happy, both mentally and spiritually. Take, for example, the case of two people, one whose thoughts are transformed in this way and another whose outlook is very worldly. If both are in hospital suffering from similar severe illnesses, the one with the well-trained mind can be mentally joyful and may even find the strength of mind to overcome his physical suffering, while the other, who has not changed his self-oriented outlook, suffers both physically and mentally. This, in turn, makes the physical pain greater so that there is no peace of mind at all.

Therefore, if we transform our thoughts by understanding the underlying cause of suffering as well as the kindness of all others, it will benefit us greatly because the continual difficulties and problems we face in daily life will never be a cause of suffering. Just as a traveler sets out on a long journey with sufficient food and supplies to avoid unforeseen hindrances, so should we be prepared for whatever life brings by changing our attitude; thus we shall be able to cope with any problem that may arise, and no suffering we may experience can either hurt us or greatly upset us.

Thus, there are two important aspects involved in transforming our thoughts into the awakening mind: we should recognize first that self-cherishing is the enemy to be annihilated, and second that all sentient beings are true friends whom we should love and benefit as much as possible. Although at present we do not have the ability to reach and benefit all beings, it is our responsibility to develop our minds so that we completely change the self-cherishing attitude into one of helping and cherishing others. In order to do this, we must be aware that all mother sentient beings have been most kind to us and are in true need of help. We must therefore look closely at all others and understand what they wish to have and what they wish to avoid. This is simple: all beings desire happiness and wish to avoid suffering. To be able to take from them what they do not want and give them what they need, we should prepare in the following manner:

*P*ractice a combination of both giving and taking.

The Tibetan term for this technique is *tonglen*: "giving and taking." However, during the actual meditation practice, it is said that taking comes first, followed by giving. We must first accept all the miseries and impurities from sentient beings upon ourselves because only then will they be in a position to enjoy the happiness and merit that we give them as replacement. This is like first cleaning a dirty pot before placing food in it.

Prior to meditating in this way we must do a preliminary contemplation in which we reflect on the fact that during our countless previous lifetimes every sentient being has been a mother to us at least once. By remembering the kindness of pure mother love, we generate the deep heartfelt wish to repay the kindness that they, as our mothers, have shown us.

Then, when practicing giving and taking, we first generate from the depths of our heart the strong desire to accept all the sufferings of sentient beings on ourselves. Out of this motivation we visualize all their miseries in the form of dark fumes, like heavily polluted smoke, coming from every direction, absorbing into us, and striking the self-cherishing attitude at our heart. After this, we generate the wish to replace this suffering with all the happiness and merit that we have. Such a motivation or wish should be united with a prayer toward our refuge objects— the spiritual master, the Three Supreme Jewels, and our own meditational deity (*yidam*)—for the accomplishment of all these practices. We give away our merit and happiness in the form of visualized radiant light blazing forth from our chest and all parts of our body. These rays illuminate all sentient beings and fulfill their every wish. We should repeat this many times in order to transform our thoughts effectively.

Commence taking progressively from your own side.

Until now, our sole consideration has been for our own benefit and happiness, and this has prevented our feeling genuine concern for others. Therefore, at first we may experience some difficulty in imagining or thinking about taking on the suffering of all other beings. We should begin the meditation by accepting all the difficulties that may happen to us today, tomorrow, and on into the next life. Although the prime object of giving and taking is to accept the misery of others, we train our mind by imagining our own immediate suffering. Only after our mind has become accustomed to this do we begin to take suffering from others. Just as a person who wishes to scale Mount Everest will first train on the lesser peaks, so should we practice on ourselves first.

Although in the beginning this meditation may seem difficult, eventually the pure wish to accept the suffering of others and give them only joy and happiness will arise spontaneously from the depths of our heart. In the army, soldiers practice in mock battles, and it is only after repeated training among themselves that they develop the desire and ability to defeat their real enemy.

Place these two astride the breath.

By utilizing inhalation and exhalation, the practice of giving and taking becomes easier. First, we inhale, breathing slowly and calmly, generating the motivation of accepting all the sufferings of others. They come in the form of dark fumes, which enter with the breath and dissolve into ourselves. Then, with the motivation of giving our own happiness and merit to others, we generate in ourselves pure white light, which we visualize as being exhaled through our nostrils. This radiant light spreads in all directions, giving happiness to every sentient being.

Sometimes we may have doubts and wonder what is the use of this practice and what are its results, for even though we visualize in this way, cows remain as cows, insects as insects, our happiness does not go anywhere, and the suffering of sentient beings is not alleviated: this practice does not appear to change anything. However, the essential point is that giving and taking helps to develop and train our mind, and it is through mental development that we reach enlightenment. Whether such a practice helps directly or has any immediate effect on other beings is not the primary consideration. It is by a gradual process that we develop our mind until it is fully compassionate, powerful, and wise—until it is fully awakened. At that point we shall be able to realize our wish to help less fortunate beings.

There are three objects, three poisons, and three sources of virtue.

Worldly beings regard objects in three ways. Agreeable objects are looked upon with the poison of attachment, or desire, disagreeable objects with the poison of aversion, or hatred, and indifferent objects with the poison of ignorance of their true mode of existence, emptiness. In our meditation we should imagine accepting these three poisons, the source of all misery, from every being in cyclic existence, and replacing them with the three sources of virtue and happiness: nonattachment, nonaggression, and nonignorance. This is the abbreviated final instruction.

If we seriously engage the practice of giving and taking, little harm or suffering comes to us. When it does, we accept it, and by realizing that its deep cause lies in a past unwholesome action, we transform it into the path to liberation. Just as a bird flaps its wings to fly higher and is further assisted by the wind blowing from beneath, in the same way we too are assisted by two vital forces as we develop the awakening mind: these are accepting all the trouble and suffering of others upon ourselves, and giving them all our merit, virtues, and excellent qualities, such as wisdom and compassion. We should practice this not only in our imagination, but when circumstances arise and there is a chance to help others; in fact, we must spontaneously do whatever we can to assist them. If we do not apply our practice to our everyday actions, we are being hypocritical and deceiving ourselves.

Remember this by repeated recollection.

We must be constantly aware of whether we are training our mind correctly or not. We should watch carefully for any erroneous attitudes that may arise and recognize correct thoughts so that we can utilize them to their fullest extent. It is like reminding ourselves again and again that, for example, we have a letter to write.

Practice every activity by these words.

Whatever we do, we should always practice according to these teachings. Whether we are sleeping, eating, walking, or meditating, we can maintain the practice of giving happiness and taking on misery. No matter what else we are doing, we are always breathing, so we can always continue the meditation in conjunction with the breath from our heart.

The correct motivation for every action is essential. For instance, we should not eat merely to satisfy our hunger. Rather, by remembering that this action is also a method of helping other beings, we should feel that we are eating in order to maintain strength, prolong our life, and thereby be able to fulfill our aspiration of benefiting others. In this way eating becomes a part of Mahayana practice. In fact, *all* our daily activities can be worthwhile if we use them with a similar motivation.

If we are now young and in good health, we should use our energy for inner development so that one day we may be in a position to truly benefit others. If we have the opportunity to meditate, we should not waste our time on frivolous activities. If a traveler from a country where there are few consumer items visits another country where such things are available, he should buy as much as he can while he is in that favorable situation. If he returns home empty-handed, he will have missed his opportunity and will continue to lack what he needs. Similarly, if we fail to take Dharma instructions to heart, the time we have spent hearing or reading them will have been wasted.

3

Changing Adverse
Circumstances into the Path

When the container and its contents are filled with evil,
change this adverse circumstance into the path to full awakening.

In this age of degeneration, both the environment and its inhabitants, or the container and its contents, are filled with the effects of unskillful actions committed in the past. Both natural turmoils and ignorance, the cause of suffering, now flourish. Famine, drought, floods, and ecological calamities abound in many parts of this globe, and the beings living here are afflicted with numerous problems and dangers stemming from greed, hatred, and aggression. These problems are conducive to all types of sickness, mental anguish, physical conflict, and so forth. Yet all such unfortunate occurrences result from a deep reason and cause, for we are directly receiving the fruition of unwholesome deeds that we, in this and previous lifetimes, have collectively committed. The result is that we are born into this specific era and these conditions of life, and we are all suffering together.

For those who are unfamiliar with the process of thought transformation, these difficult circumstances are a great burden and appear to be extremely unfavorable to the practice of spiritual development. However, for those transforming their outlook, especially by cultivating the awakening mind, these situations become an encouragement for the accomplishment of the practice. Whenever we face any problem or hardship, we should try to view it in the following manner: "These difficulties and ailments that I now have to endure have not arisen without any reason but are deeply rooted in my self-cherishing attitude. This has always been with me such that I have clutched at myself as if I were the most important and precious thing in the world. Because of this I have already committed many unskillful deeds, and now, when I experience obstacles, I am reaping the fruit of this nonvirtue."

Just as when we throw a rock straight up, it falls back and hits us, so too when we encounter adverse circumstances, we are experiencing the results of past unwholesome actions done because of attachment. In another text on thought transformation, *The Wheel of Sharp Weapons*,[16] it says that by committing unskillful deeds we create a sword that returns to cut us. Therefore, instead of being despondent, we should be grateful and joyous that the trouble has returned to attack and thereby demolish the self-cherishing attitude that was originally responsible for it.

Take, for example, an occasion when someone unjustly assails us for no apparent reason. Although most people would respond with anger, those who are cultivating the awakening mind would recollect thoroughly the assailant's kindness. He is neither harming nor abusing us but is helping us by demonstrating that the results of our past unskillful deeds are these very problems we are facing now. We should inwardly thank him for such kind teachings because now we know we must avoid creating any further causes for such results.

Those who harm us are like a teacher showing us the effects of our actions. His Holiness the Dalai Lama often says that our enemy is our greatest teacher, for not only does he provide us with a perfect opportunity to test the strength of our mental development, he also shows us clearly the faults of our past unwholesome actions.

Moreover, when confronted with such an interference, we should think that even though we are facing this great obstruction, many other beings must be enduring far worse. We should, therefore, produce the sincere wish to take upon ourselves their trials and sufferings. Then, although it may look to others that we are in difficulty, through our internal response to adverse circumstances, we shall in fact be pursuing a great practice of Dharma.

Utilize every immediate circumstance for meditation.

Wherever we are—alone in the mountains or in a crowded and bustling city, under whatever circumstances, favorable or not—whether others harm us or whether we enjoy perfect health and peace of mind, we should utilize all situations to speed us along the path to liberation. If we know how to meditate on emptiness, the ultimate awakening mind, we should practice it wherever we are; if we are stricken with a serious illness, we should consider how this is a way of expending the energy of past unskillful deeds. In this way we should be joyful and very satisfied. Even while we are eating or walking, if we continue to meditate, we shall always be upholding the essential practice of a bodhisattva.

A person following this advice will always be satisfied and full of energy; no matter how this person may appear in the eyes of others, his or her practice progresses constantly. Frequently, Milarepa would say:

> In any circumstance, whether I am sleeping, walking,
> or eating, I pursue my meditations uninterruptedly.

If we retain this practice of changing all circumstances into
the path, we shall automatically be purifying ourselves of all
obstacles and the seeds of past wrongs and shall simultaneously
be accumulating merit. Whether the situation seems conducive
to Dharma practice or not, it will be used solely for developing
the mind. Just as pouring kerosene on a wood fire causes the
flames to increase, likewise, once we have lit the flame of the
awakening mind, all situations will serve to strengthen it. In
fact, within the environment of this age many more targets will
be found at which to aim our practice, but we must be fully
prepared through having trained the mind well. Otherwise, if
we become completely depressed and discouraged, the study of
this practice will have been a total waste of time.[17]

Possess the four preparations, the highest of means.

The first is the preparation of accumulating merit. Cultivating
the awakening mind, meditating on emptiness, and making
offerings, prostrations, and mandalas, as included in the seven-limbed prayer, are all means of accumulating merit.

Second is the preparation of purifying the seed of wrongs.
In this instance, performing Vajrasattva meditation in conjunction with the recitation of the hundred-syllable mantra
is the main purification practice to do. Prostrations, together
with the recitation of the *Confession Sutra*, is also extremely effective in this regard.[18] If we do these practices with the highest
motivation, they definitely become a means of purification.
It is clearly explained in Shantideva's *Guide to a Bodhisattva's Way
of Life* that with the force of the altruistic aspiration to attain
full awakening for the benefit of all others, all these medita-

tive practices are effective in both purifying past unwholesome seeds and accumulating merit.

The third preparation is making offerings to spirits. All kinds of creatures—animals, spirits, humans, and gods[19]— often try to harm us. This becomes more apparent the more we meditate because our openness and receptivity to other forms of life increase. When such difficulties arise, instead of being discouraged or allowing hatred, paranoia, and the desire for retaliation to grow, we should offer them something and thank them deeply, for they too help us to liquidate the results of past deeds. To act in reprisal is an endless process and serves only to prolong our difficulties. On the other hand, if we react with patience and love, then our would-be enemy has no object for anger and will gradually calm down. So in this case, making offerings to spirits means reacting to malevolent forces with loving-kindness and compassion.

The last preparation is making offerings to the protectors of the Dharma, which includes making offerings to the objects of refuge, the Three Rare and Supreme Jewels, to our spiritual teacher, and to the Dharma protectors. At such times we should request their blessings and protection with thoughts such as those in the following prayer:

> Grant me your blessings and protection
> to assist my smooth progress on the path
> without being confronted and affected
> by any inner or outer interferences.
> Since my sole aim is to benefit others,
> may I be able to bear all miseries,
> such as sickness, poverty, and death,
> facing and accepting them all with joy.

4

Elucidating a Lifetime's Practice

Gather together the abridged quintessence of this advice.
Blend the practice of one life with the five forces.

There are five forces we should practice throughout the rest of this life as well as through all future existences. The first is the *force of motivation.* This means that we should be vigilant in every moment so that when emotional afflictions arise, we can stop them immediately. It also means that we should be intent upon reserving the three doors of our body, speech, and mind for the cultivation of the awakening mind. These two motivations should be maintained until we achieve the fully awakened state because they are the most sound basis for future activity.

The second is the *force of acquaintance:* with this we become accustomed to the awakening mind so that we are always conscious of our higher aims. By the force of strong acquaintance with this mind, we can use any circumstance, even seeing the misery of a dog's existence, to develop our higher aspiration to attain the complete perfection of buddhahood for the benefit of all others.

The third is called the *force of the white seed.* With this force we cultivate the seed of the awakening mind within us if it has not yet arisen, and we nourish and develop it if it already has. If all our actions are directed toward this, they contribute toward its development. The fourth, the *force of destruction,* is directed against the self-cherishing attitude, which is in complete contradiction to the awakening mind. It is our true enemy and should be destroyed completely. By realizing that this is the cause of all our confusion and suffering, we should try to check and eradicate it immediately whenever it arises.

The fifth is the *force of prayers of aspiration* for the path. Although our past unskillful deeds may be numerous, we can clearly see that we also have within us many virtuous seeds that have resulted from past wholesome actions. The mere fact that we have obtained this precious human life endowed with all the qualities that allow us to follow a spiritual path is obvious proof of this. Therefore, we should utilize the power of this aspiration for the path and dedicate all the virtuous conduct and merit we have created in this and all prior lifetimes, that we may remain inseparable from the practice of cultivating the awakening mind from now until ultimate realization. This constitutes the aspirational prayer.

We should understand that the enjoyment of relative happiness and comfort stems from previous wholesome actions, and thus, we should resolve to act similarly in the future so as to gather the causes for continuing pleasant conditions of life. Also, by realizing that any unfortunate occurrences are the product of past unskillful actions, we should firmly resolve to cease sowing any further such seeds.

The instruction for the Great Vehicle transmigration of consciousness is to apply those very five forces, lying in the perfect position.

The time of death, when our consciousness begins the transference to another life, is crucial, so we should be well prepared for it. This can be done by means of the five forces, although here they are of a somewhat different nature from those applied during our life. The first is the force of the white seed. When we realize that we are soon to leave this existence, we should prepare by discarding every one of our objects of attachment. This should be done by donating all our wealth and possessions as charity to others, or giving them to a deserving spiritual cause. To do this is very beneficial because then, at the time of death, strong craving or attachment, which would only bind us more tightly to cyclic existence, will have little opportunity to arise.

With the force of prayers of aspiration we should make offerings to the Three Supreme Jewels and our spiritual master. We should not be content with giving material objects; the best offerings to make in this instance are the seeds of all the virtuous merit that we have ever accumulated. This is most pleasing to the objects of refuge. When we make such offerings, they should be conjoined with a prayer such as the following aspiration for the path:

> Now, and at all times, through my death, the intermediate stage, the next and all subsequent incarnations, bless me never to be apart from this practice. May I always be guided by true spiritual teachers who repeatedly lead me to cultivate the awakening mind.

With the force of destruction we should first understand that the primary cause of continuing to spin through the wheel of existence is grasping at our self, wealth, relatives, possessions, and friends. Once we recognize that this clinging is our greatest enemy, we should try to eradicate every trace of such attachment constricting our chances of freedom.

With the force of motivation we should have the strong intention, as death approaches, to carry on the practice of generating the awakening mind, even through the intermediate stage between death and birth. If we make this firm intention, then the awakening mind will arise spontaneously, even though normally at a time like this there is no such freedom of action.

We should also be prepared with the force of acquaintance and be especially familiar with the awakening mind. This should be done in the "perfect position," lying on the right side with the cheek supported in the right palm and the ring finger closing the right nostril. Then, while we are still breathing, we should practice giving and taking instead of wasting our breath. Alternatively, we can meditate on emptiness, the ultimate awakening mind, by reflecting that the true nature of all that exists, both inner and outer phenomena, is their emptiness of true, substantial self-existence. Even if things still appear to our senses in a wrong way, we should consider that ultimately they are empty of this false manner of appearance.

Another thing we should take into consideration when we die is our surroundings. Although most people think there should be many people around when they die, it is actually far better for few to be present. To be surrounded by weeping and mourning will only provide external agitation disturbing our mind and, in fact, may be quite harmful. It is for this reason that Milarepa prayed:

> May I pass away where none surround me
> and where no one weeps or mourns for me.

At the time of death we should not be so foolish as to worry about whether our body will be safely taken care of by others. Once our consciousness has departed and our body has become a corpse, not only will no one want to keep it, everyone will want to throw it away!

If we pass from this life in a state of mind strengthened by the five forces and these preparations, it is certain that we shall have a fortunate and advantageous rebirth. Thus we can practice the transference of consciousness alone, instead of depending on the assistance of a spiritual master. However, if we lack this ability and our entire lifetime has been wasted in nonvirtuous conduct, then when death approaches, it will make no difference how many last rites are performed; they will be unable to weaken the results of the law of cause and effect of actions, which is strict and extremely powerful.

All Dharma collects into one intention.

All methods of the different traditions of the Dharma that were taught by Buddha Shakyamuni have the same intention and goal—the destruction of both the self-cherishing attitude and self-grasping ignorance. If we approach this goal steadily, our practice is progressing well, but if nothing is bringing these real targets closer to destruction, something is wrong in our approach. If this is the case then, just as we would add weight to one side of an unbalanced scale to bring it to equilibrium, we should add more energy to our practice by applying the appropriate methods and meditations more diligently than before.

107

Retain the two witnesses of foremost importance.

The first is the external witness of other people who observe our outward behavior and appearance. If our practice is developing well, others will judge us by our actions and will easily see whether our Dharma has been taken to heart or is merely on the tip of our tongue. If we are truly practicing, our gross emotional afflictions will decrease and our outward behavior will improve. However, this witness is not fully reliable because it is possible to deceive others by outwardly spouting clever words and pretending to be meditating and studying, while inwardly not engaging in any practice at all.

Therefore, the second witness is our spiritual master, who embodies the Three Supreme Jewels and who is not separate at all from the intrinsic nature of our mind. If we are aware of this inner witness, who understands everything that is to be known, we shall realize that this witness is more strict and exact than the external one. If we are fully confident in the purity of our motivation and have no reason to feel ashamed in regard to this inner witness, this is a certain sign that we are truly following the teachings. However, if our practice is superficial and we deceive others into thinking we are sincere, we shall be concerned that the outer witness will see through our pretension. In this case we have convinced one witness, but not the most important one. Both should be present and undeceived.

The most essential thing is actually to practice by applying the truth of the teachings to every aspect of our life. Although learning Dharma is virtuous conduct, it is insufficient. We must meditate and cultivate the awakening mind continually. The Dharma is like food: we gain no benefit from merely looking at it. To receive its full value we must digest it through meditation and integration into our lives.

5

The Measure of Having Transformed One's Thoughts

Through the successful transforming of our thoughts, significant indications will occur that will give us a gauge by which we can measure the degree of attainment in our practice.

One is always accompanied by only joyful thoughts.

If we experience a joyous feeling, even under very adverse situations, this is a sign of attainment in our practice. For example, when we meet another person who unjustly criticizes us, or when we are deeply suffering from an illness or great remorse and, instead of becoming hurt and feeling upset, we spontaneously feel great joy, this is a clear indication that we are becoming well acquainted with the principles of thought transformation. When we are not in contact with such adverse circumstances, then of course we feel happy, calm, and peaceful. Yet if we suffer and become upset just like anyone else when meeting with such difficulties, this clearly shows our practice is deficient and that we should apply still more effort. We do not require an external teacher to determine the effectiveness of our practice since we can each make our own test by assessing our reactions to the specific circumstances we encounter.

A reversed attitude indicates a transformation.

A further measure of familiarity with the practice is a change in our usual attitude toward others. Prior to this, even though we may have understood intellectually that the self-cherishing attitude was wrong, we still continued to think that we were more important than others; in our daily activities the self-cherishing feeling continued to arise spontaneously. However, a time will come after transforming our thoughts when our old attitude will be completely reversed and replaced by an attitude that always cherishes others as more worthy of respect than ourselves. When this attitude arises involuntarily in all our actions, it is a sign that our mind has become completely accustomed to this inner realization.

For instance, suppose two people arrive at a pleasurable resort they both enjoy equally only to be told that there is room for just one. The person who spontaneously feels that the other should stay and that he himself will leave—in other words, the one who considers the other to be more important—is the one whose mind is well accustomed to this practice.

There are said to be five great signs of acquaintance with the practice of thought transformation, likened to five types of great being. The first type is the *great-minded one*. Our usual habits are such that whenever an opportunity arises, we waste our time talking and thinking about mundane topics and irrelevant involvements. However, a person who is great-minded totally devotes all her time to the development and cultivation of the awakening mind.

The second type of great being, a *great holder of restraint*, is a person who, out of deep conviction in the law of the consequences of actions, continually protects himself from any unskillful deeds by mindful awareness, discipline, and pure ethics. The third type, a *great ascetic*, is a being who is fearlessly prepared to undergo any difficulty or hardship in order to subdue and destroy the force of karmic propensities and their causes, the emotional afflictions. The fourth type, a *great saint,* is a person whose actions of body, speech, and mind are never separated from the development of the awakening mind. finally, the *great yogi* is the person who cultivates the awakening mind if it has not yet appeared and increases that which has already developed, never allowing it to regress. If we become like these five great beings, it is another sign that our mind is becoming well accustomed to the practice.

One is trained if one is capable, even when distracted.

A person in deep meditation is less distracted by outer situations, and any emotional afflictions tend to lie latent. When we can remain unmoved by desire and aggression, even though distracting circumstances conducive to such afflictions arise, we have attained control over our mind, further indicating our acquaintance with the practice. It is similar to learning to ride a horse. Initially, we have to hold on tightly, but after our acquaintance and skill grow, we no longer have to worry about falling off. In fact, we will be able to eat, talk, and even sleep while riding.

6

The Commitments of
Thought Transformation

There are eighteen commitments, or precepts, concerning what should be accomplished in the practice and what should be avoided. It is worthwhile to keep them constantly in mind and to consider them as our guide when we are apart from our personal spiritual master.

Always practice the three general points.

1. The first of these general points is that we should not contradict any pledges we have made. There are many major and minor obligations concerning thought transformation, and if we consider the infraction of one to be insignificant, we are contradicting our precept. If, for example, after having learned to cherish all other beings, we casually kill a small ant and think that it does not matter, we are breaking a rule of our practice. These precepts are beneficial for all, and like the directions on a bottle of medicine that tell us the quantity and manner of taking it, these commitments clarify what assists and what opposes our practice. We should know them well, keep them strictly, and apply them exactly.

2. The second general point is that we should never allow thought transformation to become a cause for developing arrogance. The text actually says that we should not become

a "supernatural force," which is explained in the following manner. Often near trees and water there live spirits which, if disturbed, can be harmful. People who are aware of this, therefore, exercise care not to interfere with them, and avoid cutting down trees and digging the ground at such places. We might consider that such precautions are only for superstitious people and that strong practitioners like ourselves need not observe them. As a result, we might cut down trees that should not be cut, agitate and pollute water that should remain tranquil, enter an area of plague, or even eat food that is contaminated. This would be a grave mistake. All such arrogant deeds committed with the conceited thought that the strength of our practice renders us invulnerable to the consequences of such actions are contradictory to the practice. We should never be like a person who not out of compassion but out of arrogance visits someone with a contagious disease, thinking, "I'm immune to this because of the force of my mental development." Actions like this are a contradiction to the training.

3. The last of the three general points is that we should not fall into one-sidedness. We should not accept some beings into our practice and exclude others. For example we should not discriminate between a human being and a dog who both try to harm us, practicing patience only toward the human and retaliating against the dog. We should not make distinctions between human beings, favoring those who are wealthy and socially important over those who are poor and miserable. In short, we should practice equanimity toward all beings of the six realms of existence.

Change your attitude while remaining natural.

4. To cultivate our mind spiritually means for us to work constantly to transform incorrect attitudes. Until we attain complete realization, we should cultivate thoughts that hasten the development of wholesome qualities. But while we progressively change our motivation, we should continue to blend our behavior with that of others; it is unnecessary to be conspicuous. We shouldn't alter our habits ostentatiously to show that a great inner change has occurred when actually there has been only a slight modification in our thoughts.

Speak not of the shortcomings of others.

5. We should never accuse, criticize, or try to seek out and exaggerate the faults of others. However, we can offer advice so that others will understand the advantages of acting more skillfully in the future. It is another contradiction to our practice if we speak with the intention of praising ourselves while accusing, mocking, or belittling others. Since these points are easy to understand, we should not ignore them, but should apply them to our daily activities.

Think not about whatever is seen in others.

6. We should cease intentionally watching and waiting for faults in others but instead be aware and ready to judge whether our own deeds are correct or incorrect. When we walk along a dangerous cliff, we do not pay attention to what is happening around us but watch our step in case we fall. In the same way, we should focus our attention inward:

even if we accidentally notice bad attributes in others, we immediately should think that such a judgment is based upon a mistaken visual or auditory perception.

Purify first whichever affliction is heaviest.

7. All beings within the cycle of rebirth suffer to a greater or lesser degree from emotional afflictions, but different individuals have different specific afflictions that predominate. Our main defilement may be desire, aggression, arrogance, jealousy, or ignorance. We should look within and judge which one is the most serious and then apply the necessary opponent forces to purify it first.

If attachment or desire is most intense, we should meditate specifically on impermanence and the impurity of the body. If hatred and aggression dominate, we should cultivate love. If it is ignorance or blank indifference, we must meditate on emptiness and cultivate intelligent awareness. For pride and arrogance, we meditate on impermanence, the suffering of our own life, cyclic existence, and especially the misery of the three lower unfortunate realms. If jealousy predominates, we should practice rejoicing in the virtues of others. Our afflictions are countless, and since they are active in no other place than within us, their destruction can only take place internally.

Give up all hope of reward.

8. When we work to develop the awakening mind, all our efforts must be dedicated to the benefit of all sentient beings. Our practice is impure if we hope for personal gratification and reward. Such hope is not only selfish but is useless and should be renounced. Our personal benefit

is a natural side effect from sincere practice of Dharma performed for the good of all beings.

Abandon poisonous food.

9. When we know that the food we relish is tainted with poison, we reject it immediately. In our practice we must be sure that any wholesome conduct is not tainted by the twin poisons of the self-grasping ignorance and the self-cherishing attitude. If the former infects our practice, we should immediately apply the antidote of meditation on emptiness. Should our practice be stained by the latter, we should cultivate the altruistic mind and compassion.

Do not serve the central object leniently.

10. This does not mean that we should not act kindly or gently toward other beings, but that we should not be lenient toward our emotional afflictions. It is entirely due to our indulgence in the afflictions of greed, aggression, and ignorance that we remain caught in the net of confusion. Hereafter, we must stop being gentle with these true enemies and be gentle instead with other sentient beings.

Be indifferent toward malicious jokes.

11. When someone ridicules and insults us, we should not retaliate by returning the sarcasm and slander, but practice patience instead.

Do not lie in ambush.

12. When troops are unable to defeat their foes in open combat,

they often wait in ambush, using guerrilla tactics to surprise and defeat their enemy. It is contrary to our motivation to act like this toward those who have harmed us, waiting with a grudge for a suitable opportunity to retaliate.

Never strike at the heart.

13. We can deeply harm someone by callously using spiteful words that penetrate to their most vulnerable point. We should cease trying to harm either humans or nonhumans, such as spirits, by malevolent speech or harmful mantras.

Do not load an ox with the load of a dzo.

14. The dzo is a very strong Tibetan animal similar to the yak, used for heavy work such as ploughing and transporting goods over long distances. If an ox is given the load of a dzo, it cannot carry such a great burden. In other words, we should not unload our responsibilities onto others who are not capable of carrying them. In the same way, we should not pass on a difficult task to someone who is slightly stupid and does not realize our malicious intentions. Such an action will only relieve us temporarily of a responsibility that will reappear with even more strength in the future. The law of causality is unfailing.

Do not compete by a last-minute sprint.

15. We should not be like a person who, for most of the time, works with someone else to accomplish a task but near the finish shows exaggerated zeal in order to receive alone full credit for the work. This would be like two soldiers having jointly defeated the enemy, but one pretending to be the

sole hero of the battle in order to collect the medals and promotion for himself alone.

Do not be treacherous.

16. We should never withdraw slyly at the beginning of a competition and allow the opponent to think that he will win, knowing full well that this maneuver will eventually bring the victory to us.

Do not bring a god down to a devil.

17. If, while we are supposedly generating the awakening mind, our emotional afflictions increase, the god has been brought down to the level of a demon. If we are practicing properly, however, it is impossible for this to occur.

119

Do not inflict misery for possession of happiness.

18. Inflicting misery on others for the sole purpose of satisfying our own desires for pleasure and happiness is obviously contradictory to our practice.

All these incorrect attitudes only help to reinforce our own self-cherishing, and as such they are the very thoughts we are trying to eradicate. To encourage them is in complete opposition to our spiritual endeavors.

7

The Instructions on
Thought Transformation

1. Practice all yogas or activities by means of the one yoga.

None of our daily actions such as eating, speaking, sleeping, and walking should be wasted. All can be turned toward one action—the development of the awakening mind. Generally, we waste time in pointless gossip that often becomes the cause for emotional afflictions to arise in both ourselves and others. When cultivating the awakening mind, our time would be put to better use discussing the means of benefiting others and leading them beyond sorrow. Eating is usually an opportunity to satisfy mere craving for food. In this practice, however, we should keep in mind that we eat to maintain our body only so that we may achieve complete awakening and thus be in an effective position to benefit others. Out of ignorance, attachment, and pride we often wear ostentatious clothing that serves merely to demonstrate to others our false concept of a self-sufficient ego-identity. Instead of such vain self-centeredness, we should be unpretentious and simple, remembering that clothing is only meant to protect us. Also, we are usually unaware of the process of breathing. However, when it is combined with the practice of giving and taking, our breathing becomes a further means of transforming our thoughts. In such a way, we can wisely utilize every moment for inner development.

2. Practice every suppression of interference by one thought.

We should integrate all methods of destroying and expelling the interferences that arise in the course of our practice with the essence of thought transformation. Often, we shall have to bear malicious attacks from other people, animals, and spirits. At such times, instead of retaliating, we should keep our higher motivation in mind. As they too are sentient beings with feelings like ours, we should respond with only loving-kindness. When the internal obstacles of intense afflictions arise, we should recall that previously we have always given them full freedom; it is this that has held us in the tedious cycle of existence. We should not continue to repeat these mistakes but should halt their flow by applying the appropriate opponent forces.

122

3. There are two duties: at the beginning and the end.

Every morning when we rise, instead of planning pointless activities that waste our time, we should resolve to turn all actions of our body, speech, and mind toward the cultivation of the unsurpassable awakening mind. At the end of the day, we should meditate on the actions we have performed and try to recollect them all. If we have benefited either ourselves or others, we should rejoice and dedicate any merit toward the ultimate benefit of all. If, on the contrary, we have spent the day in useless activities, we should take caution against repeating such actions and make the decision to work from now on with more awareness and intelligence.

4. Endure whichever situation arises, either good or bad.

Whether we encounter difficulties and are deprived of opportunities or we obtain everything we need, we should patiently tolerate both by recollecting the constant fluctuations of cyclic existence. When wealth abounds, and we enjoy a good reputation and health, instead of immersing ourselves completely in this opportune situation, we should recall the impermanence of all things. We cannot rely on mundane perfections. Rather we should apply ourselves to the Dharma, which is trustworthy and deeply beneficial. At other times, when we meet with misfortunes that may deprive us of even the basic necessities of life, we should not become despondent; instead, we should firmly resolve to gain complete release from this deceptive round of existence by generating the awakening mind.

5. Guard both points more preciously than your life.

The first point is the general advice of Dharma practice to refrain from committing the ten unwholesome deeds. The second point refers to the specific commitments regarding thought transformation and generating the awakening mind. In order to abandon this self-cherishing attitude completely, we should constantly keep the vow of cherishing others. When we follow the Mahayana path, we must hold both these points more carefully than we would our own life. In a situation where we have to choose, we should be willing to sacrifice our life before abandoning the Dharma. It is true that in this way our brief life will be lost, but the consequences of relinquishing the awakening mind are far worse. Although we might gain some temporary benefit, we shall not be able to escape the more extensive misery of the three unfortunate realms in the future.

6. Practice the three hardships.

It is difficult to recognize when emotional afflictions arise, it is difficult to turn them away and suppress them, and it is difficult to sever their continuity. Only by meditating earnestly shall we be successful in overcoming these three hardships.

7. Attain the three principal causes.

Three principal causes are required to achieve complete freedom from suffering: receiving spiritual guidance from a master who will reveal the undistorted path to liberation; attaining a virtuous state of mind that has the will to enter the path by applying the necessary effort for meditation; and attaining enthusiasm and intelligent wisdom. Intelligence is a prerequisite for gaining understanding, but without right effort we fall into laziness. These are the three main causes of circumstances conducive to Dharma practice.

8. Meditate on the three undeclining attitudes.

124

We must have undeclining devotion toward our own master, undeclining joy and happiness in cultivating and radiating the awakening mind, and the undeclining wish to help all sentient beings, down to the smallest insect.

9. Possess the three inseparables.

The three doors of our body, speech, and mind should remain inseparable from wholesome actions leading to happiness and joy.

10. Always practice with pure impartiality on all objects.

Afflictions such as desire and hatred may manifest in relation to either animate objects such as friends, enemies, or strangers or in relation to inanimate objects such as dwellings, scenic places, clothes, and possessions. Without being one-sided, our practice should apply equally to both these categories of objects.

11. Cherish the in-depth and broad application of all skills.

We should learn to apply the skills that generate the awakening mind in such a way that they encompass the totality of all beings and all appearances. Every being throughout the six realms should be an object of loving compassion and kindness, and any sensory experience should be inseparable from the process of thought transformation.

For example, when viewing a drama or film that includes scenes of warfare and death, we should contemplate the fate of those people of the past who have actually met their death under such miserable conditions. In fact, the suffering they endured did not necessarily cease with their death but perhaps became even more intense in their subsequent rebirths. When we are watching or reading about leaders and heads of state, we can reflect on how their whole lives are wasted in the pursuit of vain goals, and remember the importance of the skillful use of this short lifespan. Movies and television can also be a potent reminder of the illusory appearance of all phenomena, and can lead us to reflect on emptiness as well.

All aspects of life present countless examples that, if we utilize them wisely, become continual opportunities to reinforce essential points in the practice.

12. Always meditate on those closely related.

When hindrances arise toward those with whom we have close relations and who have shown us much love and kindness, such as spiritual friends and parents, we should be particularly attentive. Hatred and disrespect arise easily against those who are in close contact with us; this is much more serious than when these afflictions are directed against other types of beings. Also, when we are in the company of our peers, competitors, and critics, we should take special care to control our mind. Furthermore, we must exercise awareness over our reactions toward people for whom we feel an instinctive aversion, even in cases where we do not have any personal contact with them.

13. Depend not upon other circumstances.

We should not wait for the time when circumstances are favorable and all our needs are satisfied before beginning our practice. Rather we should be able to continue inner cultivation in any situation, whether favorable or not. We should remember that within the flux of existence, everything passes as quickly as a flash of lightning. If we wait, we may find that before our plans to meditate in the "right" situation have been able to mature, our future life is upon us.

126

14. Exert yourself, especially at this time.

The opportunity to meet a spiritual master and to receive instructions, contact with the Mahayana path, the ability to generate the awakening mind, and, in particular, the freedom to practice Dharma are conditions that are extremely difficult to gather together. Even in worldly matters of little importance, no one will ever pass up a unique and fortunate opportunity when it presents itself. Thus, if we have the chance created by these conditions, we should not allow it to slip by without using it wisely.

15. Do not follow inverted deeds.

To show great patience for the difficulties of mundane affairs and not for the practice of cultivating the mind-essence is inverted patience. To have great determination to be involved in meaningless worldly diversions but no strong inclination to practice Dharma is inverted will. To revel in the enjoyment of pleasures that result from desire, hatred, and other mental negativities but not to savor the flavor that comes from meditation experience is to enjoy the inverted flavor. On the one hand, not to feel any pity for a worldly person who externally appears to lack nothing but who does not develop in a spiritual way and yet on the other to feel compassion for those who are materially poor but who sincerely practice Dharma is to have inverted compassion. To lure others, especially our family and friends, into mundane involvements that only bind them more securely to the cycle of birth and suffering instead of trying to guide them toward Dharma principles is to have inverted loyalty. And to rejoice in the misfortunes that arise for those we dislike yet be indifferent to the actions of those who benefit their fellow beings through their Dharma practice is to rejoice for inverted and wrong reasons.

127

The practitioner who applies these points to his or her own life does not have to be someone who wears the robes of a monk or nun or who lives in retreat in the mountains; the person whose actions are beneficial for himself or herself and others is one who is truly putting effort into the Dharma.

16. Do not be erratic.

Our practice, if it is to continue to progress, should be like a steadily flowing river. Intermittent practice will never lead to any firm insight.

17. Do not underestimate your ability.

We should cease weighing our capacity for doing a task and then recoiling from work we consider beyond our capacities. When we are deeply involved in the practice, we should not shirk responsibility. Instead, we should unhesitatingly give ourselves to any beneficial task, no matter what it might be. We should be like warriors and face any task without a trace of fear or reticence. However, in the initial stages of practice, it is unwise to grasp at what is overly difficult, for the mental inability to cope may lead to unnecessary depression and discouragement. Yet as we develop our mind, it is important to eradicate all delusions of incapacity that we may harbor.

18. Be liberated by these two: examination and analysis.

The essence of examination is trying to judge which mental afflictions arise more frequently and are stronger. The essence of analysis is trying to recognize the objects that provoke the afflictions to arise. Thus, by these two methods we should apply ourselves to preventing the arisal of any defilements and thereby gain liberation from them.

19. Do not be boastful.

To have practiced only slightly yet to boast pretentiously to someone else as if it were a great achievement is contrary to our practice and must be avoided.

20. Do not retaliate.

We should ignore any harmful or hateful actions directed against us, and instead of retaliating we should practice patience. In the same way, we should not keep close track of someone's harmful actions against us, repressing our anger momentarily while accumulating desire for future revenge.

21. Do not be fickle.

We are being inconsistent and fickle when initially we have much devotion and love for our spiritual friends and then suddenly develop dislike and disrespect for them.

22. Do not wish for gratitude.

When we benefit others, we should always do so with a pure mind, entirely dedicating every action so that those we help, as well as all other beings, may ultimately benefit and receive merit from this action. This should be our sole wish, without ever entertaining the thought and hope to receive thanks or praise in return for what we give.

129

Conclusion

The following are a few points the Kadam master Geshe Chekawa mentions regarding his own experiences.

Before practicing I examined my expanding actions;
then because of many of my wishes,
having undergone suffering, insults, and criticism,
I requested the instruction for taming self-grasping.
Now if I die, I have no regrets.

In a spirit of complete dedication, without any regard for his own suffering, Geshe Chekawa endured many hardships, insults, and criticism in the course of receiving the teachings on the means to tame self-grasping. Having learned this method and having applied it to developing his mind, he became free from any anxieties or regrets about facing death.

The various means for developing the awakening mind and transforming one's thoughts are like the entrance to a treasure house; from it many further ways of developing spiritual insight will arise. These practices clearly show a means of transforming any action of our body, speech, and mind into inner development. In this time of rapid changes in the world and emotional instability, this text is easily understood and is of practical benefit. Everyone wishes for permanent peace free from all suffering, yet such peace can only come from within each of us. It cannot be gained by material means no matter how extensive. Geshe Chekawa's teaching contains a supreme method for acquiring happiness; in order to attain it, however, nothing is more important than putting this method into practice. Only then will the sacrifices and efforts of a life in the quest for peace and joy be fruitful.

This concludes the text of and commentary to the *Seven-Point Thought Transformation*.

APPENDIX

Thought Transformation in Eight Stanzas

composed by the great spiritual friend of the Kadam tradition

Langri Tangpa Dorje Senge

a disciple of Geshe Potowa, who was in turn a direct
spiritual son of the layman Dromtönpa,
Atisha's closest Tibetan disciple

❖ *Thought Transformation in Eight Stanzas*

Being determined to accomplish
the highest welfare for all beings,
who excel the wish-fulfilling gem,[20]
I shall constantly hold them dear.

When in the company of another,
I shall view myself as the lowest of all
and in the depth of my heart
shall hold others dearly, as supreme.

Examining my mental continuum
throughout all actions,
as soon as a mental affliction arises,
endangering myself and others,
by facing it I shall strictly avert it.

When faced by a being of wicked nature
who is controlled by violent wrongs and sufferings,
I shall hold this one dear, so hard to find,
as though discovering a precious treasure.

When others, out of jealousy,
treat me badly, with abuse, insults, and the like,
I shall accept their hard words
and offer the victory to others.

When someone whom I have assisted
and in whom I have placed great hope
inflicts upon me extremely bad harm,
I shall view that one as my supreme spiritual friend.

In short, I shall offer benefit and bliss to all mothers,
in this actual life and in the future continuum,
and secretly I shall take upon myself
all of the harms and sufferings of my mothers.

Furthermore, having not defiled all this by the stain
of preconceptions of the eight worldly concerns,[21]
and by perceiving all phenomena as illusory,
free from attachment, I shall be released from
bondage.

Notes

PART ONE: THE JEWEL ROSARY OF A BODHISATTVA

1. A *mahasiddha* is an accomplished meditator who, through sustained practice and confidence, has gained insight into the true nature of reality. Traditionally there are said to have been eighty-four mahasiddhas of ancient India.

2. Heruka, also known as Chakrasamvara, is the name of one of the main male tantric deities. It can also refer to any male deity of the highest tantra and therefore is synonymous with buddhahood.

3. *Dzogchen* (Skt. *mahasandhi*) is a term for the highest meditative system developed in the Nyingma tradition.

4. See Geshe Sonam Rinchen, *The Thirty-Seven Practices of Bodhisattvas*, Ruth Sonam (trans.), Ithaca, N.Y.: Snow Lion, 1997.

5. See Brian Beresford (ed.), *Mahayana Purification*, Dharamsala: Library of Tibetan Works and Archives, 1978.

6. The eight worldly concerns are: gain and loss, fame and disgrace, praise and blame, pleasure and pain.

PART TWO: THE SEVEN-POINT THOUGHT TRANSFORMATION

7. See *The Precious Garland* (Nagarjuna), translated by J. Hopkins and Lati Rinpoche with A. Klein, in *The Buddhism of Tibet*, Ithaca, N.Y.: Snow Lion, 1987.

8. In ninth-century Tibet during the reign of King Ralpachen, terms being translated from Sanskrit into Tibetan were standardized in the dictionary *Composition in Two Sections*.

In this dictionary we find the Tibetan breakdown of the Sanskrit term *bodhisattva* as follows: "*Bodhi* means pristine *(byang)* consummation or full awakening *(chub)*; *sattva* means courageous mind *(sems-dpa')* or a mind acting with great strength. Thus a bodhisattva acts with one-pointed bravery and without reticence to accomplish unsurpassable full awakening." See *Tibeto-Sanskrit Lexicographical Materials,* edited by Sonata Angdu, Leh: Rinchen Tondub Tongspoon, 1973, p. 38.

9. The adamantine posture, or *vajra asana*, is described and explained more fully in many other meditation texts. The reader is referred to *How to Meditate* by Kathleen McDonald, Boston: Wisdom Publications, 1984.

10. The eight freedoms are: the freedom from birth in a hell realm, as a hungry ghost, as an animal, or in the realm of gods; in the human world, freedom from birth as a barbarian, from possessing a defective body or mind, from birth as an irreligious person who holds on to incorrect beliefs, or from birth during a "dark age" or in a "dark place" where there is no teaching of a fully awakened being.

11. There are five endowments that are beneficial in terms of each of us as individuals. These are: to be born as a human being, to be born in a land where the Buddhist teachings flourish, to possess perfect organs and senses, to be free from having committed any of the five heinous actions— killing one's mother, killing one's father, slaying a saint *(arhat)*, wounding an awakened being, and causing a schism between the followers of the Dharma—and to have faith in the three divisions of Buddhist teaching *(Tripitaka)*. The remaining five endowments are also of benefit in terms of

others: living during a time when a buddha has appeared, when he has taught the pure doctrine, when the teachings are stable and flourishing, when there is a monastic community following these teachings, and when there are patrons and realized masters mercifully supporting the doctrine.

12. See Geshe Rabten, *The Preliminary Practices*, Dharamsala: Library of Tibetan Works and Archives, 1976, 1982. Also, for a more detailed explanation of Vajrasattva, see Brian Beresford (ed.), *Mahayana Purification*, Dharamsala: Library of Tibetan Works and Archives, 1978, and *The Tantric Path of Purification* by Lama Thubten Yeshe, Boston: Wisdom Publications, 1995.

13. The quotation comes from chapter 24, stanza 11, of the *Namaprajna-mulamadhyamakakarika*, in Tibetan *dbu ma rtza ba'i shes rab*.

14. The hearers (*sravakas*) and solitary realizers (*pratyeka buddhas*) are Hinayana practitioners whose primary aim is to attain liberation (*moksha*) from cyclic existence for themselves. It is said that after they attain this state, which for them is beyond sorrow (*nirvana*), the Buddha will appear to them and induce them to take birth again in order to follow the Mahayana path and attain the fully awakened state of buddhahood.

15. This discussion appears in the eighth chapter of the *Bodhisattvacaryavatara*, translated by Stephen Batchelor et al. as *A Guide to the Bodhisattva's Way of Life*, Dharamsala: Library of Tibetan Works and Archives, 1979.

16. See Geshe Dhargyey et al., *The Wheel of Sharp Weapons*,

Dharamsala: Library of Tibetan Works and Archives, 1980; and Geshe Lhundub Sopa with M. Sweet and L. Zwilling, *Peacock in the Poison Grove: Two Buddhist Texts on Training the Mind,* Boston: Wisdom Publications, 2001.

17. According to Jamgon Kongtrul in *A Direct Path to Enlightenment,* translated by Ken McLeod, Vancouver: Kagyu Khunkyab Chuling, 1974–76, there are two verses added here with the following commentary:

> *The unsurpassable protection of emptiness is to see the manifestations of bewilderment as the four kayas.*

"Generally, all appearances, but especially these adverse conditions, are like dreaming that you are being burnt by fire or carried away and ruined by a flood. Mind holds as real these manifestations of delusion which are not real. You should determine that, although there are appearances, there is not even an atom's real existence. When you are immersed in the state of 'just appearing, but not grasping' in which there is no clinging to these mere appearances, you should understand that they are in essence empty, Dharmakaya, yet their characteristics are clear, Nirmanakaya; that this double nature is Sambhogakaya; and that the inseparability of all these aspects is the Svabhavikakaya. This pith instruction to settle in a state divorced from grasping directly at cessation, duration, and origination points out the four perfect bodies. It is the unsurpassable key instruction that cuts off manifestations of bewilderment and is called 'the armor of view and the protective circle of emptiness.'"

18. See Brian Beresford (ed.), *Mahayana Purification*, Dharamsala: Library of Tibetan Works and Archives, 1978; and Geshe

Jampa Gyatso, *Everlasting Rain of Nectar: Purification Practice in Tibetan Buddhism,* Boston: Wisdom Publications, 1996.

19. "Gods" *(deva)* here refers to beings who abide in the higher realms of sensual pleasure, still within the bounds of cyclic existence. It is said that it is very hard for them to practice Dharma since their karmic abundance of sensory gratification makes it very difficult for them first to perceive suffering and then to generate the wish to be free from it.

APPENDIX: THOUGHT TRANSFORMATION IN EIGHT STANZAS

20. The wish-fulfilling gem is a mythological jewel that, when obtained, is said to bring to its possessor all that may be desired in the world.

21. See note 6.

Editor's Acknowledgments
in the First Edition

This work has been made possible only through the kindness of many people. The commentary to the *Seven-Point Thought Transformation* was given by the venerable Geshe Rabten, a holder of the direct oral transmission and an accomplished meditation master from Sera Monastic University, one of the three great monasteries formerly near Lhasa, Tibet, and now reestablished in South India. Geshe Rabten's teaching was given to a group of Western disciples in Dharamsala, India, and translated by Gonsar Tulku. A French translation of this has been prepared by Georges Driessens.

The commentary to the *Jewel Rosary of a Bodhisattva* was given by the venerable Geshe Ngawang Dhargyey at the Library of Tibetan Works and Archives, and translated by Sharpa Tulku. It is published here with the kind permission of the Library's director, Mr. Gyatsho Tshering. Thanks go to Jonathan Landaw and Alexander Berzin for their suggestions in the rendering of the English and deepest gratitude to Lama Thubten Yeshe for making this publication possible.

May the transmission of this rare jewel open the minds of all to the infinite potential within.

About the Authors

Geshe Rabten (1921–86) was born in Dargye in eastern Tibet. He studied at Sera Monastery in Lhasa, where he gained renown as a great scholar, debater, and meditation master. In 1959, he escaped to India, where he became the spiritual teacher of Lama Yeshe and Lama Zopa Rinpoche. In the mid 1960s Geshe Rabten was appointed as a religious assistant to His Holiness the Dalai Lama. On His Holiness's request he began teaching Dharma to Westerners in Dharamsala in 1969, and he went to live and teach in Switzerland in 1974. He founded Rabten Choeling Center (originally Tharpa Choeling) in Switzerland in 1979, where he lived and worked as spiritual director until he passed away in 1986.

Geshe Ngawang Dhargyey (1921–95) was born in Eastern Tibet in the Trehor district of Kham in 1921. He took novice vows at Dhargyey Monastery and studied there and at the local Sakya monastery, Lona Gompa. At age eighteen, he went to Lhasa, Tibet's capital, to study at Sera Monastic University, taking full ordination and spending twenty years deepening his knowledge of the classics and tutoring students of his own. In 1959, he fled Lhasa in the wake of the Chinese invasion and spent nine months on an arduous journey by way of Mustang in Nepal to join the Dalai Lama in exile in India. Completing his geshe degree there and helping establish the educational curriculum for exiled Tibetans, He was appointed by His Holiness 1971 to teach Western students in Dharamsala at the newly established Library of Tibetan Works and Archives. Under his tutelage, many among the first generation of Western students of Tibetan Buddhism were introduced to its teachings. After a year as a visiting professor at the University of Washington in Seattle on his first trip to the West in 1982, he traveled the world giving teachings. Following this tour, students in Dunedin, New Zealand, requested him to establish a Buddhist center there, and in 1985, on the advice of the Dalai Lama, he moved to New Zealand, where he lived until his death in 1995.

Also Available from
Wisdom Publications

BUDDHISM
One Teacher, Many Traditions
His Holiness the Dalai Lama and Thubten Chodron

"This book will reward those who study it carefully with a deep and wide understanding of the way these traditions have mapped their respective visions of the path to enlightenment."
—Bhikkhu Bodhi, translator of *In the Buddha's Words*

ESSENTIAL MIND TRAINING
Tibetan Classics, Volume 1
Thubten Jinpa

"Anyone intrigued by the potential to bend our minds in the direction of greater clarity and kindness will find great satisfaction in *Essential Mind Training*."
—Daniel Goleman, author of *Emotional Intelligence*

THE MEANING OF LIFE
Buddhist Perspectives on Cause and Effect
His Holiness the Dalai Lama

"Studded with jewels. *The Meaning of Life* brings together the theory of Buddhist teachings and the practice of ordinary life. The Dalai Lama's exposition—thorough, gentle, and precise—reflects the depth and breadth of his training, communicating the living quality of the tradition."
—*Shambhala Sun*

Transforming Problems into Happiness
Lama Zopa Rinpoche

"A masterfully brief statement of Buddhist teachings on the nature of humanity and human suffering. This book should be read as the words of a wise, loving parent whose sternness underlines the importance of what is being taught."
—*Utne Reader*

Wisdom Energy
Basic Buddhist Teachings
25TH ANNIVERSARY EDITION
Lama Yeshe and Lama Zopa Rinpoche

"Two highly accomplished Tibetan Buddhist teachers bring alive the rich tradition of Buddhism in a way that is directly relevant to modern life. Filled with profound wisdom and useful advice, *Wisdom Energy* is a lucid introduction to the key principles and practices of Buddhism."
—Howard C. Cutler, MD, coauthor of *The Art of Happiness*

The Door to Satisfaction
The Heart Advice of a Tibetan Buddhist Master
Lama Zopa Rinpoche

Lama Zopa's message is simple: you can stop all problems forever and gain perfect peace of mind by practicing the thought-training methods explained herein. Open this book and open the door to a timeless path leading to wisdom and joy.

About Wisdom Publications

Wisdom Publications is the leading publisher of classic and contemporary Buddhist books and practical works on mindfulness. To learn more about us or to explore our other books, please visit our website at wisdompubs.org or contact us at the address below.

Wisdom Publications
199 Elm Street
Somerville, MA 02144 USA

We are a 501(c)(3) organization, and donations in support of our mission are tax deductible.

Wisdom Publications is affiliated with the Foundation for the Preservation of the Mahayana Tradition (FPMT).